T0285259

THE
TRANSFORMATIONAL
LEADER

MATT MAYBERRY

THE TRANSFORMATIONAL LEADER

HOW THE WORLD'S BEST LEADERS **BUILD** TEAMS, **INSPIRE** ACTION, AND **ACHIEVE** SUCCESS

WILEY

Published by John Wiley & Sons, Inc., Hoboken, New Jersey.
Published simultaneously in Canada.

For general information on our other products and services or for technical support, please contact our Customer Care Department within the United States at (800) 762-2974, outside the United States at (317) 572-3993 or fax (317) 572-4002.

Wiley also publishes its books in a variety of electronic formats. Some content that appears in print may not be available in electronic formats. For more information about Wiley products, visit our web site at www.wiley.com.

Library of Congress Cataloging-in-Publication Data is Available:

ISBN 9781394220328 (Cloth)
ISBN 9781394220335 (ePub)
ISBN 9781394220342 (ePDF)

Cover Design: Wiley
Cover Image: © Aranagraphics/Shutterstock
Author Photo: © Kara Nixon

SKY10069806_031824

Contents

Preface: Great Leadership Transforms Everything

LEADERSHIP ROOTED IN a genuine desire to drive lasting change and inspired by something greater than personal achievement has the potential to transform everything. In addition to the apparent benefits, such as increased production and inspiring others to attain peak performance, extraordinary leadership can help us transform entire companies, cities, states, and even the world.

Critics will claim this perspective is unrealistic and impractical, but they're missing something. They fail to recognize that humanity's most outstanding achievements are sparked by men and women who envision a brighter future and work tirelessly to make it a reality. Time and again, ordinary people placed in extraordinary situations step up to rewrite history and change the world, forging their legacies in the process.

Even though Martin Luther King Jr. endured hate, ridicule, and threats, he defiantly stood on the steps of the Lincoln Memorial in August 1963 and altered the nation's trajectory with four words: "I have a dream." As an Albanian-Indian Catholic nun in her forties, Mother Teresa had few resources and even less name recognition until her mission in Calcutta cemented her legacy as one of the 20th century's most remarkable people. As president of the United States, Abraham Lincoln exhibited resolute determination by abolishing slavery against the backdrop of a nation engulfed in civil war. He left an indelible mark on the nation's destiny by issuing the Emancipation Proclamation, a historic declaration affirming that "all persons held as slaves . . . . are, and henceforward shall be free." Nelson Mandela never deviated from his beliefs and refused to be silenced, leading to his 27-year imprisonment and subsequent election as South Africa's first black president. Legendary college basketball coach John Wooden transformed UCLA's basketball program and redefined coaching excellence at every level of sports. Despite being the winningest college basketball coach in history, his desire and ability to influence players truly set him apart.

I'm not suggesting that influential leaders must be world-renowned, larger than life, or change the world, but that said, anything can happen when you enter the sphere of influence known as transformational leadership. A great example is Rebecca van Bergen, the founder and executive director of the nonprofit organization Nest. Under her leadership, Nest became committed to advancing the causes of global workforce inclusivity, women's well-being, and cultural preservation. Van Bergen embodies the principles of transformational leadership: inspiring followers with a strong vision, challenging them to think creatively, and providing a supportive environment. Her many accolades and awards demonstrate her ability to inspire others and foster change. Her vision for a more inclusive economy and her commitment to innovation and learning underscores her effectiveness as a transformational leader.

It takes more than one person to turn around a struggling company, transform a good school district into a great one, or build a sports dynasty, but it often starts with one transformational leader.

You may say, "That's all good, but I'm nothing like these individuals. There's a reason they are who they are." Every great leader struggles with similar thoughts at some point. Still, as we proceed through this book, I will help you identify and develop your unique leadership style so that you can facilitate transformative change within yourself, your team, and your organization. It's time you see the possibilities and impact you can have right where you are.

Transformational leadership goes far beyond a job title or position. Whether you lead a business team, aspire to rise through the ranks, become an influential voice, or are a coach, teacher, or stay-at-home parent, if you want to impact those around you, keep reading.

Transformational leadership is more than a buzzword; it's a powerful way to galvanize teams, inspire action, and lead organizations and individuals toward unprecedented success. In this book, I'll unpack the principles of transformational leadership, and we will explore how to harness them to ignite change and reach new heights.

A study published in the *XIMB Journal of Management* underscores the power of this leadership approach; it revealed that teams under transformational leaders show a performance increase of 78.1%.[1] Research conducted at the University of Central Florida found that three in four employees agree that transformational leaders support a healthy work-life balance, and more than half agreed that their skills have improved under this leadership style.[2] When Walden University's College of Management and Human Potential examined the impact of transformational leadership on Global Virtual Teams, it found a positive correlation between transformational leadership and employee productivity. The study also found that employees motivated by this leadership style impact organizational growth.[3]

When we look at these studies, many envision the business world, but transformative leadership is a powerful tool often used in schools to achieve positive outcomes. According to a study published in the *Journal of Instructional Psychology*, educators who practice it often see higher student engagement with course material and other school pursuits. When discussing school management, the article reveals that "subordinates of transformational leaders have less role conflict, higher task performance, and higher satisfaction with a task than [those] with non-transformational leaders."[4]

These statistics are a testament to the power of transformational leadership, but they're just the tip of the iceberg. Behind each number are countless stories of individuals and teams who've been inspired, empowered, and transformed. There are stories of organizations that have shifted from struggling to thriving, from mediocrity to excellence. You may ask, "How can a leadership style have a substantial impact?" Well, the magic of transformational leadership lies in its core attributes: idealized influence, inspirational motivation, intellectual stimulation, and individualized consideration.

Over the last decade, I've been obsessed with leadership and organizational development, working with hundreds of corporate leadership teams, transforming underperforming teams into top performers, and coaching executives to become the leaders their organizations need. I have witnessed firsthand what can occur when exceptional leadership answers the call.

My passion for transformational leadership isn't just professional; it's personal. I've been on both sides of the leadership equation. My life has been profoundly impacted and irrevocably altered by a few individuals who never gave up on me and sparked a sense of hope that enabled me to discover my inherent greatness. I've also been the unengaged member of a team yearning for more and the struggling leader searching for a better way to inspire and make a difference. These experiences fuel my mission to help others discover the power of transformational leadership. Why? Because great leadership changes everything. It changes how teams work and organizations operate; most importantly, it can change you as a leader, team member, and individual.

In the coming chapters, I distill a decade of real-world experience and research into a comprehensive, seven-part guide. In Parts I and II, we'll examine the ever-evolving nature of leadership, discuss practical ways to overcome barriers, and work to better understand the mindset required to lead successfully. In Part III, we'll dissect and crystallize the definition of *transformational leadership*, a term that many use but few understand. Part IV emphasizes the importance of self-growth and development, further detailing the foundation of leadership. Part V delves into the intricacies of leading and the honor of helping others reveal their best selves. In Part VI, the focus is on building high-functioning teams. Finally, in Part VII, we'll address the importance of impacting the greater good rather than pursuing narrow, self-serving interests.

Transformational leadership isn't just about managing teams; it's a revolutionary philosophy that redefines the very core of *leadership*. In much the same way, this book is more than just a guide; it's a call to action that challenges you to step outside your comfort zone; create a culture in which everyone feels valued, heard, and inspired; and nurture an environment of shared vision and purpose. Essentially, it's an invitation to bring out the best in yourself and others.

That's the journey ahead, and it won't always be easy. There will be challenges, obstacles, and moments of doubt, but remember, transformative leadership changes everything. That promise alone is worth the commitment.

PART

I

Dismantling
the Leadership Crisis

1

The Catastrophic Leadership Crisis

When written in Chinese, the word crisis *is composed of two characters. One represents danger and the other represents opportunity.*

—John F. Kennedy

IF YOU'VE EVER experienced a summer day in Chicago, you know it's magical. With clear, blue skies and a gentle Lake Michigan breeze, locals and visitors alike stroll the paths of Millennium Park, the air filled with children's laughter and the distant melodies of street musicians. The first day of summer in 2022 was no different. The weather was beautiful, and I was in Chicago finishing the manuscript for my second book, *Culture Is the Way.* I had just returned from a speaking engagement in Los Angeles to conduct one of the final interviews for the book. I was scheduled to meet with Horst Schulze, cofounder of the Ritz-Carlton Hotel Company, and was looking forward to the conversation. One of my favorite aspects of writing a book is meeting extraordinary leaders and hearing firsthand how they've achieved such incredible success.

I anticipated a straightforward discussion with Schulze about building culture and embedding values as behavioral norms. However, the conversation took an unexpected turn when he shared a perspective that has stuck with me ever since. "We are currently experiencing a leadership crisis," Schulze stated. This statement reframed the entire conversation, elevating it from routine to revelatory.

It didn't seem unusual during the interview because I was preoccupied with finishing on schedule. When I reviewed my notes later that day, I became fixated on the statement, so much so that I underlined it three times. Since then, I've invested countless hours into understanding the meaning of those seven words. On longer flights, I'd take pages of notes to decipher the statement's potential value for leaders who want to make a lasting impact.

The Real Crisis

Leadership, as we know it, is extinct. Much of what we thought we knew about management and leadership was wrong; thankfully, it no longer applies. Leadership has been synonymous with using people to build your organization and rise to the top. Once there, it became about inflicting your will by enforcing a command-and-control management style on those around you.

Many leaders still use management competencies learned early in their careers despite changing workplace dynamics. As a result, they fail to engage the hearts and minds of those they lead, forcing their people to pursue new opportunities in search of belonging and fulfillment. Sadly, ineffective leadership is a widespread problem that affects nearly every field, not just business. Let's look at a few examples of outdated leadership:

- A school district requires students to memorize antiquated material that will be irrelevant in 10 years so they do well on standardized testing, which brings more federal funds into the district.
- A highly paid college coach lets their ego get the best of them and engages in unethical behavior because they believe their title and winning record make them untouchable.
- A religious leader preaches the virtues of morality and selflessness from the pulpit, but spends their free time committing adultery and coveting wealth.
- A politician secures power by telling voters they will always serve their best interests only to do the opposite by pushing the party's agenda.

We've all heard the term *crisis* used over the years, including economic, health, financial, and housing crises. Nearly every crisis, past, present, and future, can be traced to a collapse in leadership. I now know that I was so captivated by Schulze's words because they felt all too familiar. Why shouldn't they? After all, the only real crisis we've experienced is the continuous leadership crisis.

It's just that, given where we are and what we've been through, those words struck a deeper chord within me. A large part of this is that even with so much discussion about current and future crises, there is rarely an honest conversation about what shapes them in the first place. Natural disasters and many other things are beyond our control. As such, I'm not suggesting that great leadership can solve all the world's problems, but I am saying that many of our perceived crises originate from failed leadership.

The disastrous 2008 financial crisis can be traced back to failed leadership. The executives at the center of the meltdown disregarded the fundamental business principles of serving your customers exceptionally well and contributing to healthy markets.[1] Fast-forward to today, not much has changed when you look at the 2023 downfall of Silicon Valley Bank, the second-largest bank failure in U.S. history. Jerome Powell, head of the Federal Reserve, provided a transparent explanation for the collapse, saying, "At a basic level, Silicon Valley Bank management failed badly."[2]

While there have been positive and negative global changes since 2008, one thing remains consistent: failed leadership remains central to collapsing countries, institutions, and organizations. Case in point: what caused the devastating war between Russia and Ukraine? The answer depends on whom you ask. However, what doesn't is that wars are rarely waged for rational reasons. Instead, geological cleavages are often driven by the egos and emotions of world leaders. Poor and unethical decision-making is only part of the problem; we must also consider how leadership has evolved. We will explore this topic at a granular level in the following pages.

Confronting Reality

We must confront reality and start an honest, transparent conversation to build a future marked by excellence, prosperity, and unity.

Leadership isn't just a title; it's a ripple effect. Great leaders can inspire us, but bad ones, driven by ego, can wreak havoc.

Consider how just one reckless decision by a leader can destroy a nation, undo decades of progress, and harm millions of people. Much like a small group of executives at a large company can impact the livelihood of hundreds of thousands of employees with a single poor choice. And it's not just in politics or business. An unethical religious figure can cast a shadow over an entire faith, erasing the contributions of those who exemplify and live the values preached.

Failed leadership happens in public and private institutions, including the government, academia, law enforcement, and sports. Every day, we learn of another prominent figure mired in scandal. Sadly, we're so accustomed to leaders abusing power that it barely registers. However, ignoring wrongdoing or labeling it as someone else's problem only ensures history will repeat itself. Evil and chaos will always exist, but that's no reason to turn our collective heads and pretend they don't. We must make our light shine even brighter against the darkness of corruption and greed. Progress begins with confronting reality; real change starts with admitting that yesterday's solutions won't solve today's problems.

As we stare down at a rapidly evolving world, we must reevaluate the very nature of leadership. With recent strides in artificial intelligence and innovation happening at every turn, our leaders have no choice but to keep up or get left behind. If it's the latter, the cost will prove far too significant.

The Greatest Challenge

It's tough when things go in a direction we disagree with; it can leave us feeling lost and defeated. When life throws its worst at us, we must stand firm and push the boundaries of what's possible. In the past few years, tough times have touched us all, impacting some more than others. While enduring relentless hardships and setbacks is challenging, the ability to push through while maintaining hope for better days sets great leaders apart. It's been a defining characteristic of every transformational leader throughout history.

Amid the chaos, leaders who make a lasting difference dream of a brighter future and roll up their sleeves to make it a reality. This combination of vision and responsibility enables them to inspire, empower, and capture the hearts and minds of people from all walks of life. Their true power rests in this ability to unify and bring about consensus.

2

The Road Leading Us Here

Management is efficiency in climbing the ladder of success; leadership determines whether the ladder is leaning against the right wall.
—Stephen Covey

THE PATH TO this catastrophic leadership crisis was not a straight line with obvious warning signs. While the tides were already beginning to turn before the nation went into lockdown, the pandemic accelerated the timeline for many of today's most pressing leadership struggles and workplace challenges.

Before the pandemic, 61% of leaders reported receiving leadership training and support when entering a new role, compared to just 48% afterward. As a result of increased complexity, challenges, and uncertainty, support for transitioning leaders was eliminated in the initial wave of cost-reduction measures. While priorities had to shift during these disruptive times, coaching and training for leaders should not have been sacrificed.[1] What message did that send?

In 2021, the Global Leadership Forecast revealed only 11% of companies believe they have a strong leadership pipeline—the lowest this decade.[2] Although many factors contributed to the current predicament, ineffective practices and long-held misconceptions prolonged the crisis. We've glorified outdated archetypes of the leader

9

for far too long, teaching the next generation to prioritize personal success over the fulfillment, growth, and development of those on their teams.

However, in a relatively short period, we've undergone a significant course correction marked by unprecedented change, interdependence, and flux. While dwelling on the past is generally ineffective, we must explore prior shortcomings to understand how we arrived at this inflection point.

The Main Culprit

We must identify the root causes of workplace dysfunction and the leadership challenges that paralyze organizations and individuals today. As we explore these shifts, you'll notice a trend of radical advancement across nearly every aspect of life. The difference is that leadership practices fail to evolve at the accelerated rate of the rest of the world. Due to this stagnation, leaders and managers must focus on areas that do not enhance their level of impact.

Don't get me wrong, the technological innovations reinventing how we work and interact with others are crucial for progress. Still, the issue is not solely the velocity at which the world has changed over the past two decades but also the perspective and lack of intentionality in advancing workplaces and leadership archetypes.

The pendulum of digital and technological innovations causes seismic shifts across industries, resulting in many net positives. Of course, when the pendulum swings back, it reaches a new extreme in the opposite direction. When transformations occur too rapidly, they impede organizational performance and overwhelmingly impact employees and shareholders. Consider the case of Ford Motor Company.

Ford embarked on a digital transformation in 2014, launching a unique division known as Ford Smart Mobility; the goal was to produce cars equipped with advanced digital features. However, problems surfaced as the venture failed to blend with Ford's longstanding operational framework. Still, the company continued investing significant resources into the division instead of pulling back and addressing the growing issues. As a result, signs of distress spread throughout the company. The leadership team's lack of flexibility significantly impacted Ford's stock price, causing it to plummet. The company's CEO, Mark

Fields, never fully recovered professionally from the miscalculation and resigned a few years later.[3]

What good is investing in a digital platform that streamlines core objectives and changes how teams interact if leadership fails to connect with employees, foster future leaders, and promote a culture of continuous learning? Such failures make it impossible to supplement rapid change. Unfortunately, I've witnessed this exact scenario unfold across industries. Leaders become excited by the promises of innovation, products, and processes, only to be disappointed when the benefits fail to materialize. The reality is that the technology didn't fail them; they failed to innovate before implementing it. We must grow as leaders and expand our knowledge base before diving headfirst into exciting innovations that promise to bolster our pursuit of excellence.

The root cause of our crisis lies not in rapid advancement but in the stagnation of our leadership practices. We've raced forward technologically while leaving our leadership capabilities behind. To address this, we must shift our focus from adapting to the technology to transforming our entire approach toward leadership. What exactly does this require? It means strengthening connections with teams, cultivating a culture that values continuous learning, and reevaluating leadership philosophies in the face of constant change. Through these transformations, we can begin mending the issues that have surfaced in our workplaces.

Clinging to Comfort

A common leadership pitfall is returning to an emotional state of comfort—refusing to deviate from what we know and what makes us feel safest. Reluctance to let go of the familiar is the enemy of great leadership. Peace may come over us when engaging in familiar activities or returning to old habits, but that doesn't mean it's healthy. Quite the opposite. Comfort is not only the enemy of great leadership but also the death of excellence and everything we label best-in-class.

Consider the exhilaration and joy experienced early in a romantic relationship. Why does this excitement and willingness to try new things allow you to step outside your comfort zone? Because it feels good. Even if you're hesitant, there's a force that encourages you to put yourself out there in ways that may be uncomfortable. But what happens as love matures and novelty turns to regularity? Your enthusiasm and excitement for trying new things and abandoning your comfort zone gradually diminish. Those early behaviors and feelings become foreign, and your detachment from reality peaks. This growing inability to understand how we once made our partner feel loved leads to the dissolution of many otherwise happy relationships.

How can two people become so estranged and detached when they were once head over heels in love? The answer is simple in theory but difficult in practice. The longer we spend with someone, the more comfortable we become. Soon, we begin believing the solution is recreating the spark that brought us together. This idea is misguided; it fails to consider that as people grow, the sparks that keep them together must also evolve. Relying on the same magic 10 years into a relationship is unrealistic and sure to end in heartbreak.

Our current leadership crisis follows the same logic. To understand how, let's look at John, a former executive at a multinational firm. For years, John relied on a leadership style that had brought him considerable success. However, as the business environment evolved, his methods became less effective. The strategies he was comfortable with no longer yielded the same results, and his team's performance declined. After taking a significant loss on a major project, John realized that his comfort was holding him, his team, and his organization back.

While difficult initially, he began embracing the discomfort that came with growth and was soon thriving. Too many leaders today fail to recognize the critical importance of continuous evolution. Instead, they adopt the misguided belief that the qualities, skills, and convictions that got them this far will carry them further. Adhering to this false reality stunts our desire to grow and prevents us from adapting to a changing world, and it'll continue to do so. Why? Because the pull of convenience and familiarity is just too great. Chapter 4 will explore the changes required for effective leadership and discuss breaking free from the shackles of comfort.

In leadership, as in life, remaining in our comfort zones is a recipe for stagnation. The reluctance to venture beyond the familiar and push the boundaries of our abilities is what's holding us back from becoming exceptional. We must recognize the danger of clinging to comfort and seek out the unfamiliar instead. This shift requires us to constantly question our methods and beliefs, evolve with the changing times, and shed our old skin for a new, adaptive one. Let us embrace discomfort as the catalyst for growth, for it is only through this that we can truly evolve as leaders.

The Generational Shock

As the modern, multigenerational workforce shatters barriers, it's simultaneously creating silos and complexities that leaders must navigate. As if the world hasn't changed enough, we add a completely different dynamic of competing demands, including defining the future of work and widening the gap between employer and employee expectations. Each generation brings a distinct set of skills and perspectives to the workplace, but differences in opinion and values determine how each contributes to the leadership crisis.

This harsh reality frequently contradicts much of what we've learned about leadership effectiveness. Many best practices and teachings from the past were based on experience, research, and competencies that worked for decades in managerial training. The problem is that just because a generation of leaders labeled something a best practice doesn't mean it will remain so when the new generation enters the workforce.

According to a peer-reviewed study in the *European Journal of Business Management and Research,* much of this conflict stems from "younger generations viewing older generations as holding onto the status quo, [and] older generations seeing younger ones as . . . reluctant to accept things the way they really are."[4] This is why we heard so much negativity about Millennials being lazy or lacking a work ethic. However, Baby Boomers and Gen X leaders who propagated this narrative only did so because they were unable to relate to younger workers with a far different worldview. Baby Boomer and Gen X leaders who headed multigenerational teams had their ability to connect, inspire, and drive results challenged by those in emerging generations.

On the other hand, Millennials and Gen Z developed a false narrative about leadership's core tenets and the meaning of work, which exacerbated the lingering complications we've witnessed over the years. Many future leaders had their expectations distorted by this level of generational shock. Recognizing this, transformative leaders focus on nurturing and fostering leadership in others.

Take Suzie, for example. Suzie is a mid-level manager with a bright future at a national insurance company. Her employer has identified her as a future leader with high potential. But Suzie has a different take. While career-minded, she has no desire to advance by becoming a leader. Suzie's reluctance stems from negative experiences with two toxic leaders at the same company that tainted her perception of leadership. "These leaders made condescending remarks about female peers and frequently commented about Millennials not having the strength to be great leaders," she explained. I'd argue that these two individuals are anything but leaders. Still, their ignorance caused Suzie to feel marginalized and judged by her sex and generational association, doing a major disservice to their organization.

This is just one example, and far from the only one. How many other talented and potentially extraordinary leaders have been lumped into a specific generational category rather than being seen and addressed as individuals? Not recognizing that outstanding leadership is based on individual talent rather than harmful generational stereotypes is part of what defines generational shock and has contributed to our current leadership crisis. Does that mean we should ignore the differences between generations? Not at all. We must invest in generational training while acknowledging that the internal desire to make a lasting impact at the individual level fuels exceptional leaders.

Without a firm grasp of this fundamental truth, no amount of training will suffice. This alone is often why people in their 60s, 70s, and 80s can connect and inspire far better than those in their 30s. I've observed this many times; the initial assumption is that a 30-year-old is at an advantage given the dynamics of their upbringing, but this is far from the case. The heart will always triumph over the generational set.

Generational shock has brought new challenges to the leadership landscape. With a multigenerational workforce, we must learn to adapt our leadership styles to various perspectives and expectations. Rather than grouping individuals into boxes, let's see them for who they are—unique individuals with needs, aspirations, and viewpoints. Understanding and addressing these qualities will help us bridge the generational gap and foster an inclusive, productive work environment. We must not let generational shock become a stumbling block; instead, we should view it as an opportunity for growth and evolution.

The Damaging Narrative

The late political strategist Lee Atwater said, "Perception is reality." That's a problem because there's a negative perception about what it means to be a leader. That perception may be damaging and dangerous, but it's not reality.

Consider Laura, who was promoted to a leadership role at her company. She believed her new position would allow her to work fewer hours and delegate more tasks. However, she soon realized that her new role demanded more time and effort than ever before. Her team struggled under her leadership as she grappled with these misconceptions. Only after she started to see leadership as a form of service did she truly excel in her role. As Laura found out, being in a leadership position does not allow you to relax and enjoy the fruits of your labor. It's an enormous responsibility. Where does this warped idea of leadership come from? This harmful perception of leadership is often linked to gratifying the ego and self-serving mechanisms. A collapse in decision-making is inevitable when the reality of leadership as a service-driven and inspirational calling is contaminated by such false narratives.

Unfortunately, many leaders don't begin their leadership journey with a fully developed understanding of leadership as service; for them, it's a slow and gradual push. I mentioned earlier that positive and transformational leadership cannot solve the world's major problems. However, I'm convinced the world would be far better off if we eliminated this damaging narrative.

The perception of leadership as a position of privilege rather than one of service damages our organizations and is detrimental to our growth. We must debunk this harmful narrative and replace it with a vision of leadership that values service, empathy, and inspiration. This shift in perception can revolutionize how we lead and create a positive ripple effect through our organizations.

As leaders, it is up to us to challenge the status quo, rewrite the narrative, and redefine leadership in a way that inspires, motivates, and elevates those around us.

3

Rethinking the Fundamentals of Leadership

To handle yourself, use your head;
To handle others, use your heart.

—Eleanor Roosevelt

I FIRST CONFRONTED the truth about this leadership crisis while working in my office. As I stared at the countless books lining my shelves, I was drawn to those dedicated to the theory and practice of effective leadership. Amid the echoed voices of the past and present, a glaring truth hit me: our understanding of leadership, with all its traditional wisdom, is inadequate in such a rapidly evolving world. A crisis was simmering, and it demanded attention. The future, our future, hinged on our ability to redefine the very essence of leadership. At that moment, I knew we needed to rethink everything, and the clock was ticking.

Despite heart-wrenching events that've shaken us to our core in recent years, we must recognize a pivotal truth amid persistent challenges and unpredictability. Not only is deconstructing this leadership crisis within reach, but it's necessary. We cannot simply sidestep the problem, continuing our lives with the wishful thinking that someone else will solve it, or even more tragically, under the belief that the situation is beyond all hope.

Whether it's Pittsburgh or Paris, Baltimore or Bombay, people worldwide shape our future each day. Even the seconds I spend writing these words and the moments you invest in reading them mold the landscape of our collective future. Time is endless. Like it or not, today will transition into tomorrow as the future becomes the present. Whether good or bad, this moment you're experiencing will soon be a distant memory, accessible only in your mind. The march of time is inevitable.

So, why shouldn't we seize the initiative, take up the reins of leadership, and actively participate in redefining its narrative? I can't claim to know where you stand on your leadership journey, but your interest in this book signifies that you're actively pursuing ways to refine your leadership skills or aspire to be a leader.

This chapter will foster a better understanding of the core fundamentals of effective leadership and why we must work together to dismantle the ongoing leadership crisis. Our resolve and willingness to evolve will amplify our collective impact and shape the very future of leadership.

Traditional Shortcomings

Throughout my athletic career, I received recurring advice from my coaches: master the fundamentals. They made it clear that success wasn't merely about executing on game day but also putting that same level of effort into every block and tackle during practice. The thrill of victory, they stressed, was born as much from the rigors of training as it was from the heat of competition. To fans, sports at this level may seem complex and full of subtleties, a spectacle that leaves them in awe of the tactics and strategies behind each play. Yet, most sports are straightforward; beneath the veneer of complexity lies a bedrock of fundamentals players must adopt to place their team at an advantage. Games hinge on which team executes those fundamentals better. Does this guarantee a win? Of course not, but minimizing turnovers, capitalizing on opponents' errors, making every play count, and avoiding mental lapses make victory far more likely.

Sports trainer Alan Stein Jr. tells a relevant story about the late basketball great Kobe Bryant. Stein says that while watching Bryant warm up during an early morning workout, the superstar spent more than 45 minutes practicing basic footwork, such as pivots and crossovers. Bryant practiced the same fundamentals that grade-school children learn and executed every movement with precision and maximum intensity. Afterward, Stein asked Bryant, arguably the best player in the world, why he spent so much time on the basics at his level. Bryant's response: "Why do you think I'm the best in the world? Because I never get bored with the basics."[1]

Mastering the fundamentals is essential in nearly every aspect of life. Let's say your goal is to lose 20 pounds, which is challenging in a culture where nutritional advice constantly changes, and fad diets dominate the news cycle. Thankfully, you can rely on the core fundamentals of healthy living to stay focused and make progress. Some of these fundamentals are tracking your calories, exercising, and controlling blood sugar spikes. Another example is forging the path toward financial independence. In this case, learning the fundamentals of fiscal responsibility, such as using the power of compound interest, keeping a budget, and understanding how money works, would serve you well.

The same is true for leadership. Becoming a more effective leader and maximizing one's leadership potential rests on understanding certain fundamentals.[2] These principles are grounded in robust research, empirical data, and proven success:

- Vision
- Developing strategy
- Strategic thinking
- Decision-making
- Agility
- Communication
- Influence

These are just a few of the timeless leadership principles taught for decades. The problem isn't their age; it's just that we now seldom highlight the fundamentals that drive exceptional leadership. Many leaders excel at these traditional principles but fail to achieve their full potential. As our world changes and workplaces transform, the fundamentals of leadership excellence must be recalibrated and adjusted.

The foundational principles we've explored are the building blocks of outstanding leadership. As trusted guideposts, we must recognize the need to refine them in a quickly changing world. As we master the fundamentals and embrace the inherent dynamism of leadership, we'll create a future where winning isn't measured by the number of points you score but rather by the impact you make.

The Whole Person Concept

I had the incredible honor of speaking at a world-class event in Singapore for the Million Dollar Roundtable (MDRT), a global association of the world's leading life and financial service professionals. This annual event was a memorable moment in my speaking career. I'll never forget a mentor telling me more than a decade ago that if there were ever a crucial event I could speak at, it was this one. MDRT prepares and fine-tunes its message for a global audience in the weeks leading up to the event, including hosting a rehearsal with staff and committee members from around the globe.

The topic of my talk was high performance in a rapidly changing world. During the rehearsal, I spoke about achieving excellence in a way that piqued their interest. After completing my 20-minute presentation, the committee offered feedback. They explained that given its global membership, MDRT subscribes to the "whole person concept," which is the core of its member learning initiatives and promoted in all they do; it emphasizes that fixating on professional success leads us to neglect other important areas of life. This concept resonated deeply, as obsessing over professional achievement came at great personal cost too many times. This "whole person concept" relates to a dynamic workplace shift many leaders struggle with: it's the notion that team members' personal and professional lives are separate.

The transformational leader understands that a person's personal life directly influences their productivity and effectiveness in the workplace. While such a concept isn't particularly groundbreaking in today's world, intellectual familiarity differs from implementation and execution. In my experience, many leaders still subscribe to this outdated mindset and do so at the expense of decreased motivation and output.

Disengaged workers, leaders who miss the mark, and poor performance will persist until the "whole person concept" becomes the standard. Studies show that 86% of exceptional work is inspired by leaders who use connection and appreciation to motivate their teams.[3] This concept's true power is in creating cultures where employees take pride in coming to work and don't feel they need to hide their authentic selves. Furthermore, applying this idea compels leaders to dig deeper and acquire an in-depth understanding of those they lead. A leader's ability to impact and provide employees with meaningful opportunities to grow, which directly affects productivity and satisfaction, depends on how well they know their team members.

In our quest to redefine leadership, we must remember that our team members are not merely employees but people with lives beyond the workplace. More than a philosophy, the "whole person concept" is a blueprint for building more empathetic and effective leadership. We must dispel the notion that work and personal life are separate entities and realize that the magic of transformational leadership lies at their intersection. Only when we see, understand, and honor the whole person can we truly inspire and lead.

The Inspirational Leader

No leader is less effective than one who saps morale and enthusiasm from their team. Numerous studies have shown the value of inspirational leaders.[4] After all, the benefits of inspiration for an entire organization, not just select teams or employees, can be enormous.[5] As with several other fundamentals discussed in this chapter, inspirational leadership will not surprise anyone. Nevertheless, many leaders believe inspiring others is the responsibility of those around them rather than theirs. How does this affect their work? According to an article in *Forbes*, uninspired leaders are only 9% effective, with 93% rated as the worst performers by their organizations.[6]

Several months ago, I was working with a senior leader from a prominent agriculture company as part of a monthly meeting I conducted with their top executives. This individual deeply understands the industry and is always five steps ahead of emerging trends. During our conversation, we reviewed the 360-degree feedback I'd collected from his executive team colleagues. While it highlighted his many outstanding attributes, a theme surfaced: his inability to motivate others.

It wasn't merely about his struggle to inspire; many remarked that his presence depleted the energy at meetings, and his nonverbal cues conveyed unintended messages. As we discussed these valuable insights and incorporating best practices, he said, "I don't see the need to inspire others, nor do I think it's my role. If someone lacks inspiration, isn't the real question, why are they still here?"

This misguided notion that inspiring others is not a leader's responsibility hinders their ability to bring out the best in those under their charge. All transformational leaders share the ability to inspire and ignite hope for a better tomorrow. This is particularly noticeable during transitions.

As I discuss becoming an inspiring leader, you may think that inspiring others doesn't fit your personality. Many leaders use this as a deflector to avoid becoming inspirational. Inspiring others does not require changing your nature or giving inspirational speeches; it's about understanding that intrinsic motivation brings out the best in others. The more a leader can cut through the noise and engage the hearts and minds of their people, the greater their ability to inspire. As we progress through this book, we'll cover more of these underlying factors and learn how leaders use inspiration to their advantage.

Game-changing leaders use inspiration to achieve a vision and create a future nobody thought possible. Research by O.C. Tanner reveals that employees experience 57% less burnout when inspired and given a purpose.[7] The ability of a leader to inspire is the lifeblood that fuels transformation. It's a force that transcends the confines of our roles, igniting hope and carving pathways toward a brighter future. As leaders, we must harness this power, understanding that inspiration is not a burden but a gift. Let us strive to light the path for others because the leader who inspires is the leader who truly serves.

Moral Obligation and Responsibility

Leadership entails a moral obligation and tremendous responsibility to serve, behave, and look out for the best interests of people and organizations.[8] If one significant change needed to happen in workplaces today, this would be it. This shift cascades into nearly everything else a leader does. Still, it's not a skill taught in leadership development programs or featured in the curriculum of prestigious institutional business classes.

Everything and everyone benefits from a shared understanding of the moral obligations and responsibilities inherent in leadership. It's all too common for people to rise through the ranks of an organization and assume leadership roles without fully grasping the underlying principles and ethos of superior leadership.

After a presidential election in the United States, we swear the president-elect and vice president-elect into office during an inauguration. At this ceremony, the new leader recites the presidential oath of office. The oath, which dates to 1884, is a commitment to the American people that the president will defend the Constitution and uphold those sacred duties with honor. While taking the oath of office does not ensure an effective term, it establishes a standard for the high calling of serving as leader of the free world. This sets an extraordinarily high bar of accountability, as the nation witnessed the person's commitment.

What if leaders in the workplace had to recite a version of that oath in front of their entire organization, pledging to serve, honor, and protect the people and the company's best interests? Would this miraculously solve the issues plaguing American organizations today? Unlikely. But it would lay the groundwork for a leader's moral obligation and responsibility to serve their people and organization to the best of their ability.

Leaders with a profound sense of responsibility can develop the powerful but all-too-rare ability to care. Empathy is a hallmark of transformational leadership that allows us to break down barriers, create value, shape the future, define what's possible, and help others become their best selves.[9] These leaders care about the impact of their actions and the responsibility of having others under their charge. They care about paving the way for others to discover their brilliance and commit themselves to developing the next generation of transformational leaders.

At its core, leadership is a higher calling—a commitment to the welfare of others and the prosperity of an organization. This means it's not merely a contractual obligation but a moral responsibility that requires us to prioritize service, uphold the principles of honor, and protect the interests of those we lead. As we shoulder the mantle of leadership, remember that our true strength doesn't lie in our power but in our ability to care; a caring leader is tough to defeat, impossible to count out, and always has the people's support.

Leadership Vision of Impact

Leaders and those aspiring to become leaders often envision their professional journey, but those visions are self-serving at their core. There's nothing wrong with envisioning career aspirations, financial benchmarks, and other vital goals. The problem arises when our ambitions rise above the impact we wish to have. While this applies to future leaders, many experienced leaders lack a compelling vision. There are vision-setting responsibilities in everything a leader does, including:

- Strategic vision.
- Vision for direct reports and team members.
- Vision for divisions or business units.
- Vision for the overall organization or team.

I cannot overstate the importance of vision, which begs the question: why do we develop a vision for everything except our impact? Executives spend days mapping their annual goals at off-site retreats and strategic planning sessions. Why? They recognize the value of collaboration, planning, and having vigorous debates and fruitful discussions when looking into the future. Yet, when it comes to leadership, there's a gap in how leaders envision their role.

When an organization fills a leadership position, whether a sports team or a Fortune 500 company, they ask candidates to discuss their vision, so why isn't it standard practice for leaders to craft and communicate their vision regarding the type of leader they aspire to be?

Everything that constitutes excellence and propels greatness requires far more than talent and hard work; it requires a clear vision and an emotional investment. We must develop a vivid mental image; the sharper it is, the more likely we are to manifest it. As we redefine leadership, let's put aside the false notion that it's about personal advancement and instead accept that it's about creating a vision of impact that stretches far beyond oneself.[10]

Leaders must focus on crafting a vision that outlines their aspirational path, defines their desired leadership style, and emphasizes the impact they aim to achieve. Ultimately, a leader's success is measured not by the height of their achievement but by the depth of their impact.

4

Adapting to the Evolving Leadership Dynamics

Leadership is an ever-evolving position.

—Mike Krzyzewski

NAVIGATING CHANGE AND adapting to the ever-evolving dynamics of leadership is never easy. But it's essential and more critical than ever. This brings me to an important point: Benjamin Franklin was incorrect. How does the revered founding father relate to evolving leadership dynamics? Let me explain.

In November 1789, Franklin wrote that only two things in life are certain: death and taxes. While both are unavoidable, the famous statesman neglected to mention something equally inevitable but far more common: change. How certain is the promise of constant change? So much so that Aristotle contended that time does not exist without it.

Despite its pervasive and omnipresent nature, leaders are often caught off guard when change disrupts their lives and organizations. That's the thing about change, it doesn't care if you're prepared. It simply appears unannounced, uninvited, and at the most inconvenient time. Today's leaders are more vulnerable to change than ever before.

As innovation and disruption quicken, we find ourselves in an accelerating whirlwind of transformation. PwC found that nearly 40% of CEOs worldwide believe their companies must undergo significant changes over the next decade to remain economically viable.[1] With so much change on the horizon, what type of leadership is needed?

Despite shifting dynamics, there's a possibility that those at the helm have the power to take their organizations to new heights if they understand the significance of the moment. At this historic crossroads, those in positions of authority will splinter into three distinct factions.

The first are those who refuse to evolve and cling to outdated principles and concepts; they will quickly lose creditability and influence. Next are the charismatic leaders who conflate leadership with privilege and often abuse their power. Their inflated sense of self and ability to build a cult of personality will undoubtedly win them a few minor battles. But hard times will expose their façade, causing them to lose respect and fade into irrelevance. Authentic and transformative leadership is a call to serve, and as Niccolò Machiavelli explains in *The Prince*, "When you see someone thinking more of his own interests than of yours . . . such a man will never make a good servant."[2]

Finally, there are those with the power to lead us through this crisis. This group consists of service-minded leaders willing to fight alongside their team in the trenches of change to turn the tide of war. They understand that instead of issuing directives and overseeing resource allocation, a leader's top priority is safely guiding their team across the battlefield while ensuring everyone heads in the right direction. Instead of exerting authority and indulging in self-glorifying behavior, these men and women lead with humility and empathy, encouraging those in their ranks to be flexible, tough, and compassionate.

What's the primary difference between these three types of leaders? Why will one group succeed while the other two fall short? It all comes down to accepting, mastering, and executing these five evolving leadership dynamics (Figure 4.1): constant change, situational approach, building people, interconnected impact, and soft skill mastery + producing. Let's delve deeper and dissect this.

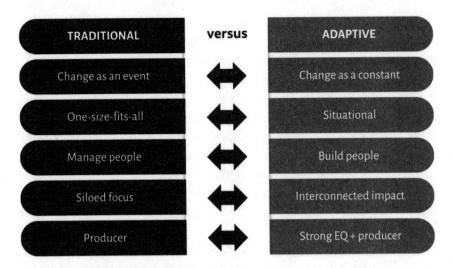

Figure 4.1   The Evolving Leadership Dynamics.

1. Change as a Constant Versus Change as an Event

For nearly two decades, leadership professionals, academics, and social scientists have researched, discussed, and debated the topic of leading change initiatives, a focus that has intensified in the past few years. However, much of the literature and beliefs surrounding this topic are fundamentally flawed. Yes, I know it's a big claim, but that doesn't make it any less accurate. The problem is that subject matter experts formed their consensus based on a model that wrongly identified change as a single, isolated event. The fact is, it's anything but a self-contained occurrence.

Early in the 20th century, philosophers Alfred North Whitehead and Charles Hartshorne developed Process Philosophy, which argued that change is continuous.[3] Their groundbreaking findings were built on the work done by pre-Socratic philosopher Heraclitus in the 5th century BC. The ancient philosopher, who influenced great thinkers like Socrates, Aristotle, Plato, Nietzsche, and countless others, held that continuous change is reality and static change is an illusion. We can observe the constant nature of change everywhere, including in a company undergoing a digital transformation, a school district launching a significant initiative, and a leader navigating their organization through difficult times.

I recently had the opportunity to work with a senior leadership team facing a combination of new management, meteoric expansion, and intensive inward restructuring. To say they were experiencing tremendous change would be an understatement. During lunch at an all-day meeting, one of the senior leaders approached me and said, "For the past year and a half, things have been a blur because of this change. When do you anticipate that things will begin slowing down?" Although familiar with the company, I don't have a crystal ball. I responded, "I honestly can't answer that question, but I have some insights I'd like to share. Do you mind if we wait until after lunch to discuss it with the entire team?" When it was time to reconvene, I took the stage, looked at the senior team members, and announced, "I'd like to deviate from my agenda for a few minutes. During lunch, Jason inquired when we could expect things to slow down and return to normal."

Everyone in the audience lifted their heads as if awaiting good news. "Things will not slow down anytime soon and never return to how they were," I explained. Following that, I abandoned my program and spent the remaining three hours listening to their concerns, answering their questions, and discussing the implications of viewing change as an isolated event rather than a permanent state of being.

While the distinction between the two is stark, we must understand that our mentality affects our behaviors, and those behaviors determine the quality of our outcome. Oprah Winfrey once said, "The greatest discovery of all time is that a person can change his future by merely changing his attitude." She's half right. It's not that our attitude is changing the future as much as how we see the world is changing us.

Good or bad, perspectives are powerful. Change may never end, but it's up to you whether you fight against that fact or embrace it—just know that only one of those options gets you where you want to go.

2. Situational Approach Versus One-Size-Fits-All Approach

In the 1970s, Paul Hersey, a behavioral scientist, and Ken Blanchard, a business consultant, developed the concept of Situational Leadership. Their theory suggests that influential leaders adjust their leadership style based on the situation and whom they're working with. It's rooted in the understanding that every person and situation is unique and therefore requires a different approach.[4] For example, an extroverted team member might thrive on regular face-to-face feedback, while an introverted team member may prefer written feedback and more time to process the information.

The flip side of the situational approach is the one-size-fits-all approach. Although this archaic leadership style is gradually becoming extinct, it's still practiced by far too many. I regularly see leaders who assume that what works for one person on their team will work for everyone else. This is a dangerous assumption and why many leaders don't achieve their desired impact. Not only does it fail to see people as individuals, but this approach also fails to consider the unique dynamics of each situation. Different tasks, goals, or challenges necessitate different leadership styles; a crisis requires a more directive, authoritative style, while a long-term project with a self-sufficient team benefits from one that allows for more autonomy.

Consider the case of Mary, the CMO of a large multinational corporation known for her charismatic and authoritative leadership style. This worked well in the early stages of the company's growth, when clear direction and a strong vision were needed. However, as the company matured, this approach became less effective.

As the team became more diverse and the challenges more complex, Mary's authoritative style stifled innovation, created tension, and bred infighting. This failure to adapt to her team's changing dynamics, culture, and environment eventually led to declining performance and low morale. Recognizing this, Mary sought advice from her direct team members, who opened her eyes to adjusting her approach based on the team's needs and changing circumstances. She learned to delegate by coaching her people more often, listening actively, and providing individualized support. Over time, Mary saw a significant improvement in her team's performance and morale. Her story illustrates the dangers of a one-size-fits-all approach to leadership and the benefits of adopting a situational approach.

Research supports the effectiveness of situational leadership. In a 2004 article in *Harvard Business Review*, Daniel Goleman discusses the work of his mentor, the late Harvard University psychologist Dr. David McClelland. In a 1996 study, Dr. McClelland made a significant discovery: leaders who can modify their leadership style outshine their less flexible peers. In his research, Dr. McClelland analyzed the performance of various division heads within a global food and beverage corporation. The results were illuminating. Among the leaders with the critical ability to adapt their styles, 87% ranked in the top third of those receiving annual performance bonuses.

Moreover, the divisions under their leadership exceeded their annual revenue targets by 15% to 20%. This starkly contrasted the divisions led by executives who could not adapt their leadership styles. Their divisions underperformed, falling short of their annual targets by an average of 20%. Dr. McClelland's findings underscore the importance of the situational approach and its potential impact on an organization's success.[5]

Yes, the approach requires adaptability and a significant investment in understanding your team and environment, but it leads to more effective leadership and better outcomes.

3. Building People Versus Controlling People

To win in the 21st century, leaders must build people up instead of trying to control them. This directive must be accepted as a behavioral norm at workplaces, athletic programs, school districts, and wherever people gather. In *The Light in the Heart*, Roy T. Bennett wrote, "Great leaders create leaders, not followers." While true, Bennett's profound observation pertains to the minority rather than the majority.

I often hear excuses like "There's just not enough time" and "I have so many other things to focus on right now." Maybe it's just me, but what's more critical than building people up and developing talent? Sadly, 9 times out of 10, it's coming from someone in an influential position. These justifications illustrate a rampant problem of men and women who are trusted to lead doing anything but.

Managing and controlling others was once considered crucial to effective leadership, but those days are long gone. Not only is this no longer an effective dynamic, but its repercussions are more damaging and toxic than anything else experienced in the workplace. I'm not implying that you shouldn't demand excellence and hold people accountable; I'm recommending that you shift your approach.

To some extent, a leader dominating subordinates feeds the illusion that they produce beneficial outcomes. Nothing destroys an illusion like the truth, so here it is: exerting your will over people backfires over time, without fail. But there's another way that relies on something other than smoke and mirrors. Transformational leaders understand that helping build up others is the backbone of excellence.

4. Interconnected Impact Versus Siloed Focus

Leaders who allocate their time, effort, and attention in a silo hinder their team's progress and harm their organization's growth. Irrespective of your role, you carry a span of control within your team or organization. While it encompasses your primary responsibility, restricting your viewpoint to this span limits your effectiveness and can stunt team growth and harm organizational culture.

Transformational leaders stand out in their primary duties. Yet, they recognize the significance of making contributions that extend beyond their day-to-day tasks for the betterment of the organization. Do you wish to broaden your influence, accelerate your growth, and make a more significant impact? Invest in building your sphere of influence beyond the parameters of your current position. This doesn't mean losing focus on the core responsibilities of your primary role. Instead, the idea is that a united and widespread leadership network is exponentially more potent than isolated leaders acting as individual contributors to influence and impact.

We're transitioning from an era of individual leaders to a time of interconnected leaders guiding the organization. The traditional hierarchical leadership model's inability to deal with today's complex organizational challenges is increasingly apparent. While organizations still require individual leaders to be accountable for their roles, superb leadership consists of groups of leaders working together as a cohesive unit to serve the organization. The capacity and performance of individual leaders will never match those of a high-performing leadership team. This new model benefits everyone involved by fostering collaboration and knowledge sharing to create a dynamic, ever-improving system of value creation.[6]

As I write this, I'm reminded of the story of Alan Mulally, the former CEO of Ford Motor Company. When he took the helm of Ford in 2006, the automaker was in a deep crisis, losing billions of dollars annually and on the verge of bankruptcy. The company's culture was deeply entrenched and siloed, with each department making independent decisions with little regard for the overall impact on the organization. The lack of collaboration and communication had created an environment of mistrust and fear.

Mulally knew that for Ford to survive, this needed to change. Instead of focusing solely on his role as CEO, Mulally extended his influence beyond his primary responsibilities to actively break down these silos and foster a culture of collaboration.

One significant change Mulally made was introducing a mandatory weekly Business Plan Review (BPR) meeting during which senior leaders reviewed company-wide performance metrics, openly discussed challenges and problems, and strategized how to move the company forward. This shift to transparent and collective leadership was in stark contrast to the previous leadership model at Ford.

Mulally also promoted a "One Ford" strategy, encouraging employees to work together toward a shared vision and common goals. He regularly emphasized that the success of one part of the organization was the success of all.

The impact of Mulally's transformational leadership was significant. Ford moved from a $12.6-billion loss in 2006 to a $2.7-billion profit in 2009 and was one of only two American car manufacturers to avoid bankruptcy during the 2008 financial crisis. The culture at Ford changed dramatically under Mulally's leadership, with the company becoming more integrated and the atmosphere shifting from fear to collaboration.[7]

What he accomplished vividly illustrates the power of transformational leadership and the importance of leaders extending their influence beyond their immediate roles. It's a testament to the power of collective leadership and the importance of breaking down silos for an organization's success.

5. Soft Skill Mastery + Producing Versus Merely Producing

The old-school mindset that success is solely determined by results is no longer applicable. Our world has changed significantly, and it's crucial for leaders to adapt. A key area for evolution is moving away from the notion that producing results alone equates to success. It doesn't. Whenever I collaborate with a new organization, I find a few teams trying to shift the culture or redefine a central tenet of its shared identity.

During the transformation phase, particular obstacles compound the inherently challenging task, notably high-performing leaders who are ego-driven or have diminished authority. Although these leaders often have good intentions, the idea that their high output allows them to do whatever they want has shaped their careers. It's not entirely their fault since organizations have reinforced this belief for decades by rewarding the behavior.

This mindset, fostered by their status as top performers, can inadvertently undermine their potential to excel and optimize their overall impact. Meeting monthly quotas, closing significant deals, or shining as a team's star performer isn't enough. An equally important factor is the value you bring to those around you and your contribution to elevating the performance of others.

The quintessence of excellence and transformational leadership lies in becoming a high performer who's mastered soft skills. This approach unlocks the potential for true transformation and maximizes impact.

PART

Conquering the Battle of the Mind

5

Shifting Perspectives: Redefining Leadership Beyond Titles and Ranks

We don't need a title to lead. We just need to care.
People would rather follow a leader with a heart than a leader with a title.

—Craig Groeschel

WHAT'S THE MARK of an authentic and transformative leader? The answer is within these four stories; read them, and we'll circle back.

In 2008, the Taliban seized control of Mingora, Pakistan. Overnight, the lives of its people drastically changed, including 10-year-old Malala Yousafzai. Along with banning television, music, and dancing, the extremists destroyed more than 400 schools and criminalized the education of females. Yousafzai's father was a teacher and education advocate who, before Taliban rule, ran a school for girls in their village. Raised to believe all people deserved equal opportunities, regardless of gender, the courageous young girl chronicled the injustices she faced for the BBC.

After fleeing to a safer region of Pakistan with her family, she became a vocal girls' education advocate. In 2012, a year after being awarded Pakistan's National Youth Peace Prize, 14-year-old Yousafzai was hunted down and shot in the head by Taliban soldiers. Incredibly, she survived. After months of restorative surgeries and intense rehabilitation, Yousafzai returned to her family, who were now living in the United Kingdom. Instead of remaining silent, she used her notoriety to amplify her cause globally. In 2014, the 17-year-old became the youngest person in history to be awarded the Nobel Peace Prize.[1]

September 11, 2001, will forever be counted among America's darkest days. Despite the heart-wrenching loss of life, the devastation would have been far worse had it not been for the courage and decisive action of those aboard United Flight 93. Authorities believed the hijacked Boeing 757 was heading for the White House or U.S. Capitol. Family members relayed this information to passengers Mark Bingham, Todd Beamer, Tom Burnett, and Jeremy Glick, who bravely fought back against the terrorists. Instead of destroying its intended target, the selfless actions of these four men forced the plane to crash in an empty Pennsylvania field, sparing the country an even greater tragedy.[2]

When Akbar Cook became principal in the fall of 2018, West Side High School had a violent reputation. Like many schools in Newark, New Jersey, constant fighting, drug use, and gang activity affected the morale and safety of its students. In addition, many in the student body faced homelessness, food insecurity, and other socioeconomic challenges that hampered their academic performance and overall well-being. Cook was not a nationally recognized education reformer or charismatic visionary with a track record of turning around failing schools. Instead, he was an ordinary person committed to making a difference in his community. As a lifelong Newark resident who'd taught at West Side for several years, Cook understood its challenges and knew the problem he'd inherit by accepting the position.

Right away, Cook made significant changes that transformed the school's environment. He used private donations to install a free laundry room in the school after learning that students were bullied for wearing dirty clothes, which led to chronic absenteeism. Realizing that his students were often hungry, Cook opened an after-school program that provided meals and a safe place to spend Friday nights. Along with these minor improvements, he showed empathy, treated students with respect and dignity, and helped them develop self-worth. He turned the school into a community hub by providing resources and fostering a sense of unity and mutual support.[3]

Cook's commitment to fostering a safe, caring, and conducive learning environment increased morale, decreased violence, and improved academic performance and attendance. His extraordinary leadership attracted national attention, including generous donations from celebrities like Ellen DeGeneres and Oprah Winfrey.

In an era of professional athletes signing eight-figure contracts and landing lucrative endorsement deals, Pat Tillman's selfless service is even more impressive. Tillman worked hard to achieve his dreams of playing in the NFL, which came true with the 1998 draft. In 2001, the 25-year-old was one of the league's top safeties and was hitting his peak—then came September 11. In a move that shocked the sports world, Tillman announced in May 2002 that he was leaving his lucrative NFL career to enlist in the U.S. Army. Despite having no previous military experience, he was determined to become a member of the elite Army Rangers and was assigned to the 2nd Battalion, 75th Ranger Regiment.

Tillman's decision was widely publicized, but he turned down numerous interview requests and insisted on no special treatment. He wanted to be just another soldier serving his country. But tragically, Corporal Pat Tillman was killed in Afghanistan in April 2004 in what was later revealed to be a result of friendly fire. Although this sparked a national controversy, it does not overshadow the remarkable character and leadership displayed by Tillman throughout his life. He demonstrated that leadership often involves personal sacrifice. He gave up a comfortable, successful career to serve his country, trading fame and fortune for the risks and rigors of military life. He did not seek the spotlight or any special recognition for his actions; instead, he hoped to contribute meaningfully to the defense of his nation. Tillman set an example of selflessness and service that continues to inspire.

While I'm sure you've heard a few of these stories before today, remember that, aside from Tillman, these individuals were not household names when they stepped up to do the right thing. But like all true leaders, their decision to make a lasting difference by taking decisive action had nothing to do with titles or what others may think—and that is the mark of authentic and transformative leadership.

Leadership Paradigm Shift

We're conditioned to believe leadership and influence require a title, position, or impressive credentials, a falsehood that has harmed countless individuals and organizations. That's because if someone does not hold the title of leader, they're unlikely to identify as one. Regardless of culture, societal norms often assign value and prestige based on title and organizational hierarchy.

Still, the foundation of transformational leadership is determined by mindset and skill set rather than credentials. This is why, throughout my years as a leadership consultant, I've witnessed those without titles have a far greater impact than those labeled as leaders.

While a title may cause others to be submissive and carefully choose their words in your presence, it does not guarantee that you have their hearts and minds. If those you're responsible for feel compelled to change who they are in your presence, I'd argue you've failed to gain their trust altogether. Still, many in positions of authority find this puzzling, especially when they report constant motivation and productivity issues. But dig a little deeper, and you'll find they know that their authority lacks influence.

Leadership is the conscious decision to make one's own life and actions impact and positively influence another human being. The real problem with relying on titles and rank is that once a leader ascends the ladder and is officially recognized by the standard norm, there is a tendency to believe that the hard work is complete. In actuality, the real work has only just begun, and the weight of that work increases with each passing second. The ability to influence and impact others while building a bigger and better future is far more important than any title or career milestone. We need to shift our leadership paradigm to align with this reality.

The Downside of Chasing Titles

I recently spoke with a mid-level manager at a company I've worked with for several years. While this leader has incredible potential, his unwavering desire to chase titles holds him back and stifles his growth. Every conversation with him concerns a new position he's attempting to collect. Yes, I said collect because, as I quickly learned, it's not the role, responsibility, or challenge he's after but the title. This manager has changed his mind about his next career move four times in the past three months alone, and each time, the focus is on a shiny new title. He explained, "I've put in 10 years of hard work for this company. It's not about the money anymore; I only need the title. Everything will be better once that happens."

You might wonder what's wrong with someone wanting recognition for a decade of hard work. As I said, the issue is not wanting the title; it's the actions and outcomes leading up to their desire for it.

Although this leader has great potential, there is a significant gap between where they think they should be and what they've produced up to that point. Some days, he's on, but other days, his performance is lackluster, and his temper gets the best of him. Each of his five direct reports has praised him, but they've also complained that he spent little time with them and provided no coaching. If there isn't an intense drive to coach and develop those you lead, inspire them, and prepare them to become future leaders, receiving a new title will not alter the fundamental requirements and responsibilities associated with the role.

As we've seen, constantly pursuing titles can backfire, harming the leader and impacting those they lead. Here are a few of the negative consequences of being a perpetual title chaser:

- Neglecting to make a daily impact where you are.
- Work becomes ego-driven rather than competence-driven.
- The focus on outcomes stifles growth and prevents you from developing into the leader you must become.
- Stress levels increase as you focus on what you can't control.
- Distorted reality clouds what's most vital.

Earning the Right

Transformational leaders are busy leading and making a difference long before they are given an official title. How others view them does not affect their desire and inherent motivation to build up those around them. They have fully adopted the mentality of working tirelessly to earn the title of leader. And most of the time, their focus is not on what they do but instead on what they inspire others to do. Not on who they become but on who they inspire and help others become.

Operating with an attitude of earning the right shifts the emphasis from pursuing a title or destination to enhancing impact and influence in the present. Focusing on interactions with those you lead and opportunities to make an impact will get you closer to your goal. Before receiving the right to be called a leader, you must earn the right to:

- Be trusted by extending trust to others.
- Inspire others by your example.
- Be praised by consistently giving others credit.
- Have others buy into an idea by fully committing to it yourself.
- Expect the most of others by setting the bar.
- Gain the support of others by offering an abundance of support.

Whether you are a leader now or aspire to be in the future, success requires developing the right mindset and never asking something of your team you wouldn't do yourself. You're on the wrong path if you believe others are obligated to never let you down because of your position. But there's always hope. Being a leader is about so much more than the title on your business card or the plaque on your door. To remain grounded, we must all challenge our ideas, motives, and perspectives from time to time. This practice ensures we're truly leading from a place of service.

When you approach leadership from a position of impact rather than of titles and rank, you'll notice things falling into place; this indicates that you're on the path to transformational leadership.

6

The Influence Factor: Projecting Influence Without Authority

Leadership is influence. To the extent we influence others, we lead them.
—Charles Swindoll

CONSIDER THIS SCENARIO: after a year in your role, you are assigned to lead a team project with 15 colleagues from your department. Although you want to prove yourself, worry and self-doubt emerge. You think, "I don't hold a management title, and many on my team have been here far longer; why would they listen to me?" These negative, demeaning thoughts get louder each day until they eventually creep in at night, leaving you wide awake.

Instead of sleeping, you stare at the ceiling, telling yourself, "You've never led a team, let alone managed an entire project. You don't have what it takes, and everybody knows it."

Whether or not you've experienced something similar, there will come a point when you must project authority and influence. Here are some examples:

- As a parent, you're responsible for acting as an authority figure, especially during your children's formative years, and influencing and guiding them as they develop positive habits they'll need as adults.

43

- As an athletic coach, you influence how players see the world and help them shift from being self-serving to developing a team-first mentality.
- As an educator, fostering and shaping a student's love of learning is critical; to do that, you must cultivate a supportive environment by influencing and uniting the community, parents, and faculty.
- As an employee in the nonprofit sector, you must educate the public, potential donors, and governmental agencies on the importance of an underlying issue and influence their support for your organization's mission.
- As a leader in the workplace, you influence those on your team and the company's direction and culture, including behavioral norms and workflow. This has an enormous impact on productivity and efficiency.

Brands worldwide spend $1 trillion annually to influence consumer behavior.[1]

Ask yourself: would they continue spending that much money if it weren't effective? Of course not! Whether you realize it or not, you're influencing and being influenced nearly every second of every day. Knowing that makes you less susceptible to what others want and enables you to be more strategic about when, why, and how to exert your influence.

Don't Fall into the Trap

If influence is vital, why aren't more people striving to be more influential within their circles? Wouldn't having a little more pull at home or work benefit them? While there are many explanations, the most significant barriers to increased influence are predicated on:

- A belief that the ability to influence is contingent on title, rank, or position.
- A failure to recognize the significance and value of being influential.

These barriers are mental traps that often dictate actions, mindsets, and beliefs concerning who should and can lead. After decades of conditioning, we believe influential people have risen through the ranks, received a title, and earned the privilege. This perspective is wrong, and it's caused severe damage by preventing many people from realizing their full potential and allowing others to abuse their authority with impunity.

This reminds me of a story I heard while traveling a few years ago. It's about John, a school janitor known for his positive attitude and ability to uplift those around him. Despite holding a low-ranking position, John was among the most influential individuals in the school.

Mr. Allen, the school's new principal, quickly noticed that the atmosphere seemed brighter when John was around and that he inspired students, teachers, and parents. Wanting to understand the secret behind his influence, Mr. Allen asked, "I've noticed you have an incredible impact even though you're not a teacher. How do you do it?" John smiled and replied, "I believe influence is based on how you treat people, not your title. Everyone can make a difference, no matter their position."

The principal was amazed by John's insight and realized he'd fallen into the trap of conflating influence and title. John challenged this misguided belief and showed him that true leadership was about character, not formal authority. Over the next six months, Mr. Allen worked with John to implement school policies and initiatives based on his leadership philosophy. This included encouraging open communication, recognizing the contributions of every staff member, and promoting a supportive environment. The transformation was remarkable; teachers felt empowered, students felt valued, and morale improved.

The story spread through the small Midwestern town, and people realized that influence was not reserved for those in positions of power but within the grasp of all who chose to lead with humility and kindness. This illustrates what happens when we remove these barriers and accept that authentic leadership is about influence, not title.

Mastering Influence: An Art, Not a Role

We've established that influence transcends role, title, and rank, but that's not all it does. This philosophy also creates transformational leaders. Regardless of their career field—sports, business, public service, or countless others—transformational leaders share an intrinsic desire to expand their impact. Sound familiar? If so, continuously nurturing this inner drive is the cornerstone of a growing sphere of influence.

The Influence Model, a framework I developed to simplify the art of influence, helps individuals elevate their leadership abilities, irrespective of their titles (Figure 6.1). It's a roadmap for those committed to enhancing their effectiveness and expanding their influence as leaders.

Let's unpack the six components of the Influence Model:

1. Head

The first step is to understand that transformational leadership has nothing to do with your title and everything to do with your ability to influence other people. We've already established this, so why am I reinforcing it? Because without comprehensively understanding this truth, your influence and impact will never grow.

When it comes right down to it, mindset is everything. What you think and the quality of your thoughts profoundly influence your behavior, which determines your outcome and impact. The problem is that perceptions, thoughts, and beliefs continuously evolve. Still, even if our thoughts change, we must recognize that our power and significance remain. If we lose sight of that, we lose crucial ground in the battle to become influential leaders.

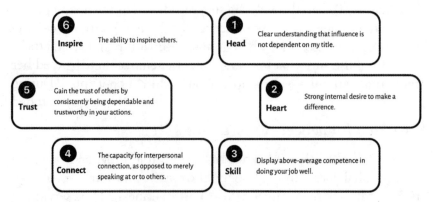

Figure 6.1   The Influence Model.

The further you travel on this journey, the more you'll see that transformational leaders value and nurture influence rather than chase status and cling to positions of power. Maintaining this discipline, focus, and philosophy will help you earn the respect and title you deserve, regardless of where you are in your career. The initial battles fought to become influential are fought and won in the mind. It all begins with believing you have the ability, potential, and significance to influence others.

2. Heart

The natural progression of influential leadership starts in the mind but quickly leads to the heart of every leader's journey: engaging their passion. Transformational leaders recognize that without a burning desire to make a difference, they will never capture the hearts of others. This insatiable hunger to make a difference is there from the start and never disappears. Do you feel it?

The chapters ahead include the stories of transformational leaders who've made an extraordinary difference. Why did I demonstrate the selflessness and passion of great men and women who weren't motivated by accolades or recognition but by a desire to effect positive change? Because it's impossible to truly help others and improve the world around you if you're not doing it for the right reasons.

A great example is Billie Jean King, a legendary tennis player who fought for gender equality in sports. Her influential leadership began with a vision of breaking down barriers and fighting for equal treatment for female athletes. She envisioned a future where talented women would receive the same recognition, respect, and opportunities as their male counterparts.

With unwavering commitment and passion, King used her platform to make a statement that couldn't be ignored. During the historic "Battle of the Sexes" match, the world watched King face off against professional male tennis star Bobby Riggs. Along with stunning the crowd with her talent, King's achievement symbolized a brighter future for women's sports and inspired millions.

In 1973, her work with the Women's Tennis Association (WTA), an organization she co-founded, resulted in the U.S.

Open becoming the first major tournament to offer equal prizes regardless of gender. King's influential leadership inspired a generation of both male and female athletes. Her legacy is a powerful reminder of what's possible when an influential leader takes a passionate stand.

As famed English author and preacher Charles Spurgeon said, "Good character is the best tombstone . . . carve your name on hearts and not on marble."

Spurgeon emphasized that investing time and talent in helping others is far more valuable than pursuing personal gain. True leadership isn't about promotions, pay raises, or increasing social status; it's about making a lasting difference. The truth is that service must be carved into your heart to be a great leader.

3. **Skill**

The third component of the Influence Model deals with an unavoidable, often uncomfortable fact: it's not enough for a leader to just set a high standard for performance; they must also meet it. I've worked with many leaders who have their heads and hearts in the right place but lack the skills to operate at the high level required for their positions. Unfortunately, while they're typically nice people with potential, they rarely succeed as leaders.

While it's not about being the most gifted, you must display above-average competence to project influence and make a significant impact. You may be able to coast along for a while, but simply being good enough will drastically diminish your influence and impact. Managers who dream of leveling up to the executive suite frequently ask my advice on advancing their careers. Whether on 5th Avenue in New York City or Main Street in Omaha, my response never changes: "Do whatever it takes to be exceptional and solidify yourself as someone who prepares, executes, and delivers enormous value."

What it means to "be exceptional" may change depending on the industry.

Still, your ability to set a high standard and overdeliver never does, regardless of where and what you're doing. If you're thinking, "This could have been first on the list instead of third," you're right. But there's a good reason it's not number one, and that reason is the talented jerk we all encounter at some point who produces incredible results but destroys everyone around them. Being exceptional is useless and potentially destructive until you have the head and heart for counterbalance. Once you do, it becomes rocket fuel.

4. **Connect**

There's a widespread assumption that all influential leaders are eloquent public speakers; this is a myth. Far more important than world-class oration is the skill of forging genuine connections, which extroverts, ambiverts, and introverts can all master. The reality is that how we communicate matters far more than what we communicate.

How often have you been impressed by someone's ability to articulate their ideas clearly or express themselves with empathy and compassion? Communicating in a way others relate to increases your influence. Practice this skill by being intentional in your interactions while keeping these three factors in mind:

- **Vulnerability:** People construct walls when communicating with strangers or in professional settings. It stems from a fear of judgment. People will more likely agree with you when you avoid building these walls by demonstrating a little vulnerability. How do you make yourself more vulnerable? When appropriate, be honest about the hardships you're dealing with. Since everyone is struggling, sharing will help others relate to you. That's what it means to be vulnerable. For instance, a leader I work with begins team meetings by acknowledging an area where he's fallen short and how he plans to avoid doing the same thing next time. He sends a strong message to the rest of the team by owning up to his mistakes instead of placing blame on them. Showing vulnerability improves his chances of connecting with others.

- **Authenticity:** Never have people been this hyper-concerned about their image. Radical authenticity stands out in a world where everyone projects a curated version of themselves that doesn't exist. Being genuine matters. What does this look like? Rather than following the crowd, set the pace and lead by example. It's one thing to know what the right thing is; it's something entirely different to lead others toward doing it.

One way to be more genuine is to take a few minutes out of a conversation with a coworker to discuss your passion or what you hope to accomplish this year. Setting limits to prevent oversharing is essential, but being open about your values and encouraging others to do the same can be powerful in fostering genuine connections.

- **Empathy:** Everyone we meet is dealing with an issue or problem. This is the most useful advice I've ever received, and it helps me show more empathy every day. Our response to a situation is drastically altered when we keep this in mind, especially when someone makes a mistake. Always try to see the best in people.[2]

5. Trust

Trust is the cornerstone of influence. Are you trustworthy and dependable? Can others count on you? Your ability to influence others is directly proportional to the trust you've earned. Trust is complex, but these questions provide a solid foundation for understanding and determining if someone is trustworthy. It governs nearly every aspect of our lives. Yes, mutual trust is the foundation of healthy friendships, but we also rely on trust to determine which brand to buy.

It's even in sports; great teams are those whose players believe the person next to them will do their job and what's best for the team.

The same fundamental principle applies to becoming an influential person. Did you answer the questions that kicked off this section with a resounding yes? If not, it'll likely limit your ability to grow your influence. Our ability to influence improves when we prove ourselves to be dependable and trustworthy. A lack of trust decimates leaders, teams, organizations, and eventually everything it touches. While many hold the title of leader, their actions create division and strife. For them, trust is nowhere to be found. They may have the title, but they lack anything meaningful and impactful.

Bill Belichick, future first-ballot Pro Football Hall of Fame inductee and former head coach of the New England Patriots, asserts that trust cannot be demanded or bought. While it can't be purchased, trust has a price; it's just that most people aren't willing to pay. That price is showing up every day, even when you don't want to, and being dependable regardless of how you feel. Although it's a price that's too steep for many, Belichick is right that trust must be earned and that the balance must be settled daily.[3]

6. Inspire

The final piece of the Influence Model is the ability to inspire. Great leadership isn't about dominance, superiority, or wielding power; it's about creating a positive environment that inspires and unlocks your team's potential. But this can be difficult, especially early in your career. The challenge isn't getting your team to achieve organizational goals—many people can do that—it's igniting the flames within so they can achieve more than they ever believed possible.

In today's ever-shifting environment, the capacity to inspire is desirable and a game-changer. Mastering the art of inspiration is the key to projecting influence and achieving long-term organizational success, whether you're an experienced leader or an aspiring one. A leader who can inspire can propel individuals toward excellence by unleashing their potential and cultivating a sense of ownership, responsibility, and accountability. Such leaders foster a positive culture and create an environment where team members feel valued, fulfilled, and confident in their abilities. A team with an inspiring leader is far more likely to thrive, develop an optimistic mentality, and consistently perform at its best.

Each part of the Influence Model framework can stand independently, but these six have a far more significant effect when combined. Remember, being inspirational doesn't mean giving motivational speeches, but discovering your unique leadership style does require intentionality. This is one of the most significant discoveries you'll make in your career.

The Choice Is Yours

You don't need a title, promotion, or recognition to start influencing others, and you certainly don't need anyone's permission to make a greater impact. Leadership is not based on how others perceive you or your number of direct reports. Instead, your commitment to serving others and shaping a better future is the true determining factor. Regardless of who notices, living a life of significance should always be your primary objective and the intrinsic motivator fueling your actions, aspirations, and thoughts. The decision is yours alone—nobody else's.

7

The Value of Continuous Self-Transformation

When we strive to become better than we are, everything around us becomes better, too.

—Paulo Coelho

TRANSFORMATIONAL LEADERS UNDERSTAND that who they were and what they accomplished two, four, or six years ago is irrelevant. There is deep recognition that where they are now will not get them where they want to go in the future. I've noticed that all transformational leaders share a drive to evolve, transform, and grow, regardless of their expertise. This defining characteristic sets them apart and makes them impossible to ignore.

When describing a great leader, it's common to list their notable accomplishments, achievements, and successes. However, we often overlook the most crucial aspect of what makes a leader great: continuous self-transformation. This ongoing personal evolution is foundational, for it's the catalyst behind every victory and success a leader achieves. Without this internal growth and relentless self-refinement, the outward milestones we celebrate would not exist.

The Truth Will Set You Free

Where we are today reflects our commitment, or lack thereof, to constant growth and forward momentum. This is a harsh reality for some, particularly those addicted to complaining, making excuses, and blaming others. But this doesn't only apply to those who aren't where they want to be; achieving enormous success doesn't exclude you from falling into the trap of complacency. How can someone successful be in danger of failing? They lose sight of a fundamental truth: within our drive for continuous self-transformation lies the essence of who we are, what we do, and the boundless potential we possess.

When we forget this essential truth, we're no longer anchored, and our inclination to coast through life and succumb to adverse external influences dramatically increases. This is as true for you as it is for me. Numerous times throughout my life, I've coasted or failed to pursue my goals.

Thinking back, I can pinpoint when I stopped focusing on self-improvement and started reevaluating my beliefs, mental capacity, and behaviors. Had you brought this to my attention then, I would've likely made an excuse or attempted to justify my actions. Nevertheless, time prepares us to face uncomfortable truths about ourselves, and the truth will set you free—but first, you must unlock the cage door.

The Epicenter for Everything Else

Think of a significant personal or professional goal you want to achieve in the next few years. Now, take 30 seconds to close your eyes and visualize it. As you sat with your eyes shut, did you notice your focus drifting to what you must do before achieving your goal? If you did, you might have also realized that your to-do list primarily consists of outward-facing tasks, like calling people, filing paperwork, raising money, winning games, and more. While these are important, we often overlook the most vital factor in determining our success: the ability and willingness to transform. Achieving a goal, forming a habit, or making a positive change requires becoming an entirely new person.

This inability to transform is the primary reason large jackpot lottery winners are far more likely to declare bankruptcy within three to five years of winning, and another one-third will file eventually.[1]

The truth is that becoming wealthy overnight doesn't turn a person who lacks financial discipline into a wise investor; it just prolongs the inevitable. Let's take Mary, for example, who earns an annual income of $51,636, which is average in the United States, but wins $50 million. Despite having exponentially more money, Mary will continue thinking like someone who earns $24 an hour. Why? Because the changes Mary experienced in her life were external, not internal.

Transformational leaders recognize that positive change begins within. You do not need a degree, credentials, or anybody's permission to focus on self-growth. All that's required is a hunger for growth, lifelong learning, and a willingness to embrace the new, improved you each day. No matter where you are today or hope to be tomorrow, committing to endless internal transformation will have a far more significant effect than you can imagine.

Deliberate and Intentional

In the 12th century, an Indian mathematician claimed to have achieved perpetual motion. Since then, history's brightest minds have debated the theory, and many have attempted to build perpetual motion machines.[2] The concept is simple: perpetual motion is a hypothetical state in which an object set in motion continues moving infinitely without additional energy from an external source. In other words, it exerts more energy than it consumes. It's the equivalent of Newton's cradle continuing indefinitely after the first steel ball crashes into the rest. But that's not what happens. Each time the balls come into contact, the friction created results in less energy transferred; it loses momentum, slows down, and eventually stops. Modern technology has all but proven perpetual motion to be impossible for much the same reason.[3]

Thankfully, the process of perpetual transformation is real, but like anything else, you must add energy to keep it in motion. That energy comes from starting each day with purpose and vigor. Transformational leaders are intentional about their approach to the day and deliberate about striving to surpass and outperform themselves. Wait, did I say that they're deliberate about outperforming *themselves*? Clearly, I meant they're deliberate in outperforming others, right? Wrong. While the rest of the world competes to validate their dilutions of self-importance, transformational leaders ignore external distractions, prioritize growth, and see each day for what it is: an opportunity for meaningful change.

In 1976, future Swedish author and psychologist Dr. Anders Ericsson earned his Ph.D. from the University of Stockholm and was ready to begin a career focused on human memory. However, a question that had long interested him would shape his career and revolutionize our understanding of mastery and excellence. The foundation of his question was: why do some people achieve extraordinary levels of expertise while others with seemingly equal opportunities do not?

This curiosity eventually drove Ericsson and his team to publish "The Making of an Expert," the 2007 article that popularized "Deliberate Practice." Published in *Harvard Business Review*, the now-famous piece contradicted English Victorian psychologist Sir Francis Galton's century-old assertion that nature determined intelligence, not nurture. After extensive research, Ericsson concluded that "experts are always made, not born."[4] He believed anyone could achieve genius-level mastery given enough time and commitment, writing, "Like [all] world-class performers, Mozart was not born an expert—he became one." As you can imagine, saying that anything is possible was controversial. After all, people go to great lengths to avoid personal responsibility and blame genetics, circumstances, and others for their shortcomings.

During his research, Ericsson studied the fascinating case of László Polgár, a Hungarian chess teacher and educational psychologist who boldly told the *Washington Post*, "A genius is not born but is educated and trained." Not only did he believe that he could make any healthy newborn into a genius, but he was prepared to prove it. He'd developed a detailed plan to raise his children long before meeting his wife. In 1965, Polgár courted a Ukrainian teacher named Klara; he wrote her a series of letters explaining his plans to turn any potential children into prodigies. Klara agreed, and they were married.

The couple's three daughters, Susan, Sofia, and Judit, began formal training as toddlers and became chess prodigies. During their careers, the International Chess Federation ranked Susan and Judit among the top female players in the world. Susan became a grandmaster at 15 years old and was the No. 1 ranked female player from 1989 until retiring in 2014. Judit, who ranked 55 before she was a teenager and broke Bobby Fischer's title as the youngest grandmaster in history, refused to compete in women-only tournaments.[5] Today, she's the only woman to have been a candidate for the World Chess Championship title or to have placed in the overall top 10. Although she's the youngest Polgár sister, Judit is considered the greatest female chess player in history.[6] László Polgár's methods may sound extreme, but they helped validate Ericsson's hypothesis.

Since the Polgár sisters, we've seen other children raised to be champions; look no further than Tiger Woods or the Williams sisters (Venus and Serena). It's important to note that in these incredible cases, success was not about putting in the hours but intentionally pushing boundaries, receiving feedback, and refining skills based on that feedback. Mindless repetition was replaced with deliberate, goal-oriented improvement. The Polgár sisters taught us a valuable lesson: we're truly architects of our reality.

Deliberate practice isn't just for genius musicians or professional athletes; it's a lifelong philosophy for anyone committed to self-transformation. Every day is an opportunity to evolve, to deliberately inch closer toward our goals, regardless of how far away they seem. Excellence isn't a destination but a continuous journey of challenging ourselves to become better than we were yesterday. The key to achieving the extraordinary doesn't lie in the hands of fate but in starting each day with intention.

Floodgate of Possibilities

Self-transformation allows us to see the world through a unique lens that increases our capacity for innovation and creativity. As a result, we gain insight, develop wisdom, and seize opportunities previously overlooked. In this way, it's like learning a new language. With practice, we understand a world that was incomprehensible—even invisible—to us prior.

When you embrace self-transformation, the floodgates of possibility are released. This means leaving our former selves behind. You wouldn't expect a butterfly to concern itself with its struggles as a caterpillar. After some determined effort, what was once an existence of crawling on branches and eating leaves becomes an endless sky of blue.

Similarly, as we transform and outgrow our previous selves, we interact with our environment in new, exciting, and empowering ways that change our potential and reality.

At its core, continuous self-transformation prepares us to adapt and thrive in a rapidly changing world. This transformative process equips us with the resilience and flexibility to tackle challenges, seize opportunities, and lead with courage and confidence. Remember, the most significant difference between those who accomplish the extraordinary and those who waste their potential isn't their starting point; it's their mindset. The extent of our success is defined by our desire for self-improvement, willingness to embrace change, and capacity to take calculated risks. Refusing to remain static entails persistently advancing, learning, and becoming your best self. That is the unwavering pursuit that fuels the extraordinary.

In many ways, it's a chain reaction—our transformation influences those around us. As we change, so do our relationships, workplaces, and communities. We inspire others to grow, strive, and transform. This ripple effect can be far-reaching and profound. It's how we, as individuals, significantly impact the world—particularly our own.

This process may be intimidating. It requires us to venture into the unknown, leave our comfort zones, and face our fears and insecurities. However, it is through this discomfort and uncertainty that we discover our full capabilities and potential.

Through continuous self-transformation, we open the floodgates of our ultimate self, setting free an endless torrent of possibilities and opportunities.

8

The Secret Formula:
Inner-Work = Outer-Impact

Every answer you are seeking is already inside of you. Look within. Do the inner work.

—Akiroq Brost

PEOPLE ARE SURPRISED to learn that football was not my favorite sport as a child, given that I played in college and had the opportunity to play in the National Football League. My dream had nothing to do with touchdowns or tackles and everything to do with bypassing college for a career in the Major Leagues. At 13, while chasing this dream, I experienced a crushing defeat when my traveling baseball team narrowly lost a critical playoff game—with it went our hopes of being champions.

My heart boiled with rage. I was furious at everything and everyone. As a young baseball player, I was a jack of all trades: pitching, playing the outfield, manning third base—I did it all. However, my talent shined brightest when I stepped into the batter's box. There was nothing like the crack of a bat or crushing a pitcher's fastball.

As a power hitter, I regularly hit home runs that sailed far over outfielders' heads. It was a point of great pride, so I took that playoff loss so hard. During the biggest game of my young life, I failed to perform—going zero for three. My temper, always my Achilles' heel, made it impossible to brush off a strikeout and head into my next at-bat with renewed focus. Not only had I blown three offensive opportunities, but I also committed two unforced errors that resulted in four runs. With each strikeout and subsequent error, I descended deeper into a pit of frustration that clouded every aspect of my game.

After the long, quiet ride home, I asked my parents to drop me off at my grandparent's house, which was just down the street from where we lived. With my uniform covered in grass stains, my face smudged in eye black, and my head hung in defeat, I slowly made my way to their living room, where my grandfather, a die-hard Chicago Cubs fan, spent evenings watching games on television. I threw myself onto the sofa and pulled my ball cap over my eyes. After two minutes of silence, he turned off the television and asked that I sit up and look at him. The words he shared with me that day soothed my wounded pride: "You have extraordinary potential, son, but if you don't learn control and work on yourself from the inside, you will never win." His wisdom transcended the game: "Becoming a great ball player has more to do with how tough you are on the inside than how far you can hit or how many opponents you can strike out. You're gifted. But you still haven't won the battle within."

Although I was too young to understand then, he knew the lesson would be invaluable someday. The philosophy behind my grandfather's wisdom is fundamental to transformational leadership, underscoring that growth, self-discipline, and personal responsibility are essential for developing influence. The intentionality and rigor we dedicate to nurturing our inner selves dictate our ability to make a lasting impact.

The Battle Within

My grandfather's influence helped shape the man I am today. Unfortunately, I never told him how much he meant to me or thanked him for putting me on the right path. But, from that day forward, I understood the value of self-improvement and what it meant to win "the battle within." Each day, we grapple with internal conflicts that attempt to destroy our self-worth, abilities, and identity. Often, these battles are wars of deception aimed at stifling potential and blurring our road to greatness.

Like everything, this begins with our mind. Research shows that most of our thoughts, around 80%, veer toward negativity. Surprisingly, 95% of these harmful thoughts are also repetitive; this broken record of negativity results in pessimistic, self-limiting beliefs that inhibit growth. It's hard enough to navigate external negativity without worrying about self-induced stress and anxiety undermining our professional performance and leading to depression, low self-esteem, and a self-defeating attitude that restricts success.[1]

However, there's no reason for this to be permanent. We can redirect our thoughts from negative to positive, turning them into tools for constructive action and self-improvement. It begins by changing our perception—because, like the late political strategist Lee Atwater said, "Perception is reality."

The Starting Point

We've established that winning the internal battle is imperative for maximizing our influence and impact. But where should we begin? The following chapters discuss the core competencies for driving leadership excellence. However, before delving into specifics and daily practices, we must identify a baseline; these three actions will help you do this regardless of where you are on your journey.

1. Foster Astonishing Curiosity

The first step is cultivating an extraordinary level of curiosity. If we lack a strong sense of curiosity, we become trapped in seeing, living, and experiencing the world as we're accustomed to. If you ask someone about the keys to successful leadership, curiosity is unlikely to make the list. But of the countless leaders I've worked with, the most transformative are committed to curiosity regardless of their income, success, or status.

The unfortunate reality of life is that the more we experience and older we get, the less curious we are. Without intense curiosity, the drive to learn and grow ceases to exist. Remember your childhood and that innate need to question everything? We must reintroduce that type of childlike wonder into our lives as it fosters consistent

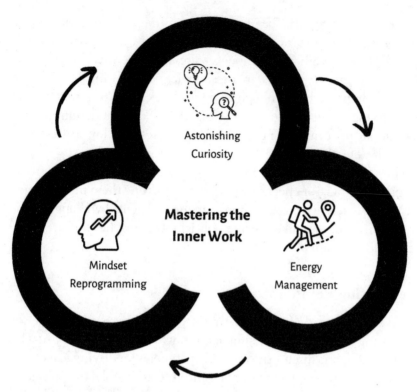

Figure 8.1   Mastering the Inner-Work.

development and lifelong learning. Here are some practical ways to bring curiosity back into your daily life:

1. **Ask questions:** The habit of asking questions and challenging everything is essential for instilling more curiosity and gaining a deeper understanding.
2. **Collect ideas:** Curious people gather ideas that intrigue, inspire, and challenge their thinking. While it's up to you where these ideas come from, beginning this habit is vital.
3. **Form a think tank:** Regularly meet with others to exchange ideas and insights because engaging with colleagues, friends, and mentors to discuss diverse perspectives is more powerful than you realize.
4. **Express yourself:** You do not need to be a professional writer to share your thoughts. Frequently expressing yourself facilitates discovery and opens a world of possibilities.

2. Reprogram Your Mindset

We must commit ourselves to reprogramming our mindset every day. As we discussed, most thoughts are negative, self-deprecating, and repetitive; having a great day today doesn't guarantee we will wake up happy and fulfilled tomorrow. If that were the case, no one with financial independence, career success, or a healthy, loving family would suffer from hopelessness and despair.

The path to exceptional leadership doesn't begin in the conference room or the corner office; it begins in the complex neural pathways that shape your mind. This is true of leadership and the inner work necessary to drive outward impact. Transformational leaders become exceptional in their minds before anyone else recognizes them as such. Similarly, champions in the sports world win in their minds long before stepping onto the field or into the ring.

Neuroplasticity—our brain's lifelong ability to reorganize itself by forming new neural connections—is well established in neuroscience. This ability of the brain to change and adapt is crucial in the process of mindset reprogramming. It allows us to reshape our brain's default thinking and response patterns. Whenever we consciously think positively, we strengthen positive neural pathways; with enough repetition, this changes how our brain functions. Therefore, we have significant control over our thought processes and, by extension, our reactions to the world around us.[2]

Consequently, understanding and leveraging neuroplasticity can be a powerful tool in fostering a growth mindset. It opens the doors to learning new skills, adopting healthy habits, and mitigating negative thought patterns. We forge and reinforce new, more beneficial neural connections by exercising our brains using meditation, cognitive behavioral therapy, visualization, or affirmations. Much like the gardener who cultivates a thriving garden by nurturing his plants and removing weeds, we curate a thought garden by focusing on empowering thoughts and systematically eliminating harmful, self-deprecating ones.

In the wise words of self-help luminary Napoleon Hill, "Whatever the mind can conceive and believe, the mind can achieve."[3] To unlock your full potential, you must become the master architect of your mind, continuously sculpting it with unwavering commitment and perseverance. Mindset reprogramming can take a variety of shapes and forms. Your journey is unique, and it's up to you to discover the best path forward. As an example, here are a few methods that have an extraordinary impact on my life:

1. **Books we read:** Have you ever heard the expression "time is money"? Well, it's not—it's far more valuable because it's the raw material of life itself. To squander it is to waste the very essence of existence. This understanding is the foundation for curating my reading list. The books I choose to immerse myself in must inspire growth, intrigue my soul, challenge my intellect, and help me hone a skill. My reading list is a repository of wisdom and inspiration that fuels my continuous personal and professional development.

2. **Podcasts we listen to:** Learning while commuting or exercising has never been easier. The advent of digital platforms has transformed downtime into a time for self-improvement. Podcasts have become a mobile classroom for absorbing the knowledge of world-class leaders, industry experts, inspiring mentors, and the figures who command our admiration. This incredible medium has endless potential and the power to spark intellectual curiosity and broaden our horizons.

3. **Stories we tell ourselves:** We each have an internal story we tell. The narrative we carry in our minds' silent corners holds immense power in our daily lives. It governs our actions, behaviors, and thoughts, whether positive or negative. But, like great fiction authors, we dictate our story—not the other way around. So, arm yourself with the pen of self-awareness and rewrite your narrative. Infuse it with optimism, resilience, and self-belief, turning your internal dialogue into a wellspring of positive energy. After all, you are the main character.

4. **Visions we cling to:** The legendary Muhammad Ali famously said, "If my mind can conceive it . . . I can achieve it."[4] A clear vision of our desired outcome is the first step toward realizing our goals. Make a daily habit of introspection, deep breathing, meditation, and visualization techniques that empower and nurture your inner strength. Regular mental rehearsals cultivate a roadmap to success and prime your mind to make it attainable.

3. Manage Your Energy

For years, boosting productivity has meant focusing on strategic time management and daily efficiency. Although this remains crucial, energy optimization fuels our performance, propels our advancement, and amplifies our influence. Detailed calendars, productivity apps, and delegating low-value tasks are the tools that shape our day, but they're not the lifeblood of our performance. Energy is.

Even the most well-intentioned efforts will falter without energy management. Time is the great equalizer—we all have the same 24 hours; what we do with it sets us apart. Consider a high performer you admire. While their productivity and efficiency create the illusion that they've bent the fabric of time and space, I can assure you that they haven't.

It has nothing to do with the amount of time and everything to do with their ability to channel energy. If they only had 15 to 20 hours daily, they'd still get more done than 99% of the population. The challenge isn't finding more time but regulating our energy expenditure; this becomes particularly important when broadening our impact and influence. Focus on these four critical pillars when pursuing optimal energy management:

1. **Master your fitness:** Today, the importance of prioritizing physical health is irrefutable. For example, Sir Richard Branson, the founder of Virgin Group, credits daily exercise as the key to his astounding productivity. In a 2019 blog post, the entrepreneur revealed, "I seriously doubt that I would have been as successful if I hadn't placed such importance on my health and fitness." Whether you engage in strength training or yoga, physical activity significantly enhances your health, mood, and daily productivity.

2. **Fuel high performance:** People striving to become top-tier leaders often underestimate nutrition's role. While I'm no nutritionist, I assess a leader's eating habits before moving on to strategy. Why? Because if you have a Lamborghini but fill the tank with cheap gas, it won't perform. In other words, poor nutrition hampers your execution and impact. Remember, the journey to influential leadership is like a competitive sport, and

not even Michael Jordan, Tom Brady, or Derek Jeter could have reached greatness without the proper fuel.

3. **Recover like a pro athlete:** Driven individuals spent much of their career in high gear, but the older we get, the more we realize this is unsustainable. However, simply being aware of this is insufficient; as with any critical area of life, you must approach recovery with a plan. LeBron James spends over a million dollars annually on health and recovery protocols.[5] I'm not suggesting you spend a fortune like "King James," but there's a reason why the best invest so much in their recovery.

4. **Identify your value rocks:** Much like an organization's core values anchor its mission, we, as leaders, must determine what we stand for. These are "value rocks," the keys that profoundly impact our sense of fulfillment and clarity. Consider Mahatma Gandhi, whose "value rocks" of nonviolence and truth defined his leadership and changed the world. Identifying and focusing on your value rocks allow you to be selective, turning away opportunities that do not align with your values.

Prioritize and Invest Daily

Embrace the guiding principle to *prioritize and invest in yourself every day*. This investment triggers a cascading effect, enhancing your personal development and the world around you. Like any investment, the benefits you reap directly correlate with your effort. Therefore, turn your attention inward and dig deep.

As you evolve internally, your external impact will grow. Let consistency act as your guide while commitment fuels your journey. The more steadfast your path, the more significant the rewards; your efforts will accumulate and gain momentum. Wherever you are on your journey, continually striving for growth brings clarity, focus, and the excitement that comes with transformative leadership. Remember, leadership isn't about holding a title; it's about making a daily choice to grow, invest in yourself, and elevate those around you.

PART

Identifying the Core Components of Transformational Leadership

9

Defining Transformational Leadership: A Framework for Change

Imagine a world where leadership isn't associated with titles but recognized for what it is: the ability to drive positive change, transform lives, and strengthen organizations. Imagine a world where the foundation of leadership isn't blind ambition, career mobility, and the pursuit of power but inspiring those around you and delivering extraordinary results. Welcome to that world.

—Matt Mayberry

IN PREVIOUS CHAPTERS, we dissected the leadership crisis, explored significant shifts within the discipline, and examined changing team and workplace dynamics. We also explored the significance of cultivating the right mindset and perspective. What has become clear is that transformational leadership is about impact and influence. It fosters significant change in leaders, organizations, and those who aim to become leaders.[1] Now, let's focus on what it means to be a transformational leader and how to use this approach to achieve your goal.

The Core of Greatness

Transformational leadership centers on inspiring and motivating others to envision a brighter future for themselves and their organizations. Expanding upon this, it's about encouraging individuals to focus on

69

making a broader, more profound impact. It's rooted in pursuing self-determined evolution rather than external validation—but we'll discuss this in more detail later. This is essential because transformational leaders adhere to universal principles integral to their identity and philosophy.

Transformational leaders:

- Prioritize self-growth over professional advancement.
- Know that leadership is a lifestyle, not a persona.
- Take ownership and never make excuses.
- Embrace reality but dream of a brighter future.
- Let actions speak because they're louder than words.
- Are consistent, reliable, and trustworthy—full stop.
- Understand that leadership is NEVER about power and is ALWAYS a tremendous responsibility.
- Demonstrate courage when others hesitate.
- Uplift and inspire in a world that oppresses and derides.
- Practice what they advocate.
- Never mistake movement for progress.
- Invest in helping other people grow.
- Commit to excellence because mediocrity isn't an option.

Unlike traditional models that rely heavily on external rewards and punishments, transformational leadership cultivates an environment where our internal transformation drives us. This shift from external validation to intrinsic motivation is crucial for fostering genuine and sustainable growth within an organization.

This form of leadership transcends industries; from corporate boardrooms to the sidelines of professional sports, the principles of transformational leadership hold true. While examining successful business leaders and athletic coaches, primarily in football, I identified striking parallels in their most defining leadership traits. I went further by distilling these down to key characteristics that successful men and women use to transform their leadership and inspire exceptionalism.

The Five Characteristics of Transformational Leadership are a blueprint for leadership and career success that can be adapted and applied in various situations. These characteristics are not just theoretical constructs; they have been tested and proven in the real world.

These characteristics, when combined with being exceptional at your craft, have the potential to bring about significant change. Transformational leaders catalyze large-scale organizational success by fostering an environment where individuals are inspired to pursue growth and free to innovate. As we delve into these five characteristics, we'll explore how they collectively form the framework for transformative leadership.

The Framework for Transformational Leadership

The following five essential characteristics are at the core of a transformational leader's unparalleled impact. These foundational traits are the pillars supporting their profound influence and success. By cultivating and implementing these attributes, you can position yourself as an impactful leader and a catalyst for enduring change and progress. These characteristics are more than just skills; they are the guiding principles that can shape your leadership journey, enabling you to leave a lasting and significant imprint in your sphere of influence.

The Five Characteristics of Transformational Leaders:

1. Talent Fanatic: Association is everything in all domains.
2. Take Ownership: Complete ownership of what's controllable.
3. North Star: Compelling vision of the future.
4. Chief Culture Driver: Culture is the way.
5. Grit: Long-term consistency of effort.

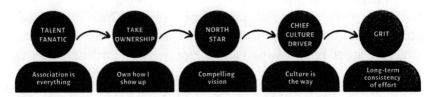

Figure 9.1 Five Characteristics of Transformational Leaders.

1. Talent Fanatic

Transformational business leaders and athletic coaches alike understand the profound importance of talent. While talent alone doesn't guarantee success, it's the foundation upon which greatness can be built. That's why great leaders in both the boardroom and on the field are unwavering fanatics regarding talent. What do I mean by *talent fanatic*? It's someone who's always thinking about talent and looking for individuals with the skills, drive, and potential to contribute significantly to their organizations or teams. Moreover, they prioritize talent development, not just through external hires but also by cultivating and nurturing talent from within. They recognize that a cohesive and committed team, united by a shared vision, can achieve feats that surpass the capabilities of a collection of highly skilled individuals. They are also always asking if the right people are in the right seats.

I regularly meet leaders who don't grasp the importance of being a talent fanatic. While many say that they value talent, their behaviors contradict these claims. Recently, I had the opportunity to work with a senior leadership team from an investment banking firm. When we started, I asked, "Who here is a *talent fanatic?*" Every hand shot up. As time progressed, I realized their answers and self-perceptions did not align with reality. Most of these leaders lacked enthusiasm for talent development; the initiatives they did have were little more than compliance measures. These included regularly coaching team members, talent calibration sessions, and ensuring information flowed between departments. While technically checking off the boxes, they approached these initiatives with lackluster effort. So, why did I use this example? Because it's representative of a prevalent, recurring pattern I've observed over many years.

Evolving into a *talent fanatic* is not just about fostering and developing talent within the workplace but also knowing that our associations and interactions touch every aspect of life. Once understood, nurtured, and enacted, greater outcomes unfold. In my experience, being the most talented individual, especially in athletics, doesn't equate to having the longest career. I've met many of these individuals who fail to rise to the top, not because they lack ability but because they associate with the wrong people. This included exceptional athletes who let others drag them down. Transformational leaders understand that who they associate with and seek advice from outside of work directly impacts their performance at work. And as one becomes more successful, more "yes" people emerge—those who tell you what you want to hear rather than what you need to hear. The core qualities of a *talent fanatic* are:

- Cultivating talent from within, attracting others who align with team objectives, and pursuing untapped potential.
- Recognizing that a talented team that lacks shared vision will never outperform a less talented team that's aligned.
- A willingness to let others receive recognition for achievements they did most of the work on.
- Deliberately form trustworthy allies, mentorships, and positive relationships with others that foster their professional and personal development.

2. Take Ownership

Transformational leaders never shirk away from taking ownership of their actions and decisions. They don't indulge in blame games or excuses when things don't go as planned. Instead, they accept full responsibility for their choices and the outcomes they produce. This ownership mentality empowers them to control the variables within their grasp and make impactful changes. Besides, failing to take ownership undermines our capacity to show up daily and contribute.

Whether a business executive facing a market challenge or a football coach dealing with a losing streak, these leaders embody accountability. They recognize that personal growth and team success hinge on their ability to control the controllable, adapt to adversity, and steer their organizations or teams in the right direction.

Complaining, making excuses, and placing blame are toxic and erode our ability to impact and effect positive change. Since "take ownership" sounds vague and generic, let's break it down into two actionable steps:

- Take full responsibility for your life and devote time, energy, and focus to controlling the variables. Be accountable and own the things within your control.

- Assume complete accountability. This is an uphill endeavor, particularly when facing adversity or less-than-ideal situations. In my experience, challenges occur daily, and circumstances often make accepting responsibility difficult, such as facing rejection or dealing with the unpredictability of others. Nonetheless, when we lose sight of complete accountability, we lose the ability to take corrective action.

Many of our concerns, anxieties, and grievances are beyond our control. In these instances, we experience dissatisfaction because we can't exert influence. Will 20 minutes of excessive worrying, followed by a panic attack, solve your problem? No, of course not. But calming down, envisioning the best possible outcome, and solely focusing on what you can control will.

The extent to which transformational leaders achieve success and make an impact is largely dependent on their readiness to accept that everything starts and ends with them. Taking complete ownership not only results in positive outcomes, but it also earns the trust of those you lead.

3. North Star

Transformational leaders stand out and see reality for what it is. They possess a North Star—a compelling vision of the future that guides their actions and decisions. This vision extends beyond personal success; it encompasses the success and well-being of their organizations or teams. A transformational business leader articulates a vision for their company, rallying their employees around a shared purpose. Similarly, a great sports coach inspires their team with a vision of victory and excellence. This shared vision is a compass, guiding everyone toward a common destination and fostering a sense of purpose and unity. I've spent more than a decade working with leaders and organizations; can you guess the one thing that's consistently absent from struggling companies? That's right, an inspiring and compelling vision of the future.

I'm not implying that these organizations were struggling because they lacked vision. But it's also not a coincidence. While most companies acknowledge the importance of vision, they underestimate its true power. Simply having a vision is not enough; it must also be enthusiastically articulated and connected to a greater purpose. This brings us to the importance of having a North Star to keep you on course. There are two functions a North Star serves on the journey to transformational leadership:

1. As a compass that guides an individual leader's compelling vision.
2. As a compass that guides an organization's or team's compelling vision.

Excluding either imposes an unnecessary restriction on expanding your capabilities and achieving significant outcomes at scale. Those with a strong vision who cannot reframe it as a shared vision severely limit their sphere of influence. Conversely, someone who fosters a shared vision but struggles with self-limiting beliefs and a lack of personal vision will also be unable to find lasting success.

Due to a desire for purpose and impact, a transformational leader embraces an expansive personal vision. Simultaneously, they dedicate themselves to articulating a compelling shared vision that inspires those around them and garners overwhelming support.

4. Chief Culture Driver

Transformational leaders understand that creating and nurturing a positive culture is paramount. They prioritize collective interests over individual agendas, egos, and aspirations, fostering an environment that promotes collaboration, trust, and excellence.

In the business world, a thriving organizational culture drives productivity and innovation. In athletics, a strong team culture enhances camaraderie and performance on the field or court. These leaders recognize that culture is the foundation upon which success is built, and they invest their time and effort in cultivating a culture that prioritizes collective excellence over individual achievement. Not a week goes by that someone doesn't ask if I miss football. If we're talking about the game itself, the truth is, not anymore. But, if we're talking about the locker room camaraderie, relationships with teammates, and coaches who invest time and effort into building a strong, supportive environment, then I do. After speaking with men and women who've retired from the military, I feel they experience something similar: they miss having such unimaginably close bonds built on a foundation of shared purpose.

One of my primary reasons for writing *Culture Is the Way* was that I recognized building an exceptional culture mattered to me and countless other leaders. Why? Because it's the driving force behind greatness and fulfills that need to be a part of something more significant than ourselves. How important is it? I've seen many top performers with limitless potential fail because of their inability to foster a collaborative environment that prioritizes collective excellence over individual achievement.

Regardless of their title, transformational leaders assume the role of chief culture driver. This added responsibility includes exerting a subtle yet impactful influence over their organization's culture, which compounds everything else.

5. Grit

I didn't write these five characteristics in order of importance because they're all crucial. However, if you pressed me for the one indispensable cornerstone, I'd unequivocally select grit. Transformational leaders understand that winning is not always about raw talent or intellect but often the relentless spirit to persevere. The pressures of leadership can take a toll on an individual's physical and mental well-being. However, these leaders possess the inner resolve to keep going when others might falter. They demonstrate a resilience that transcends adversity, inspiring those around them to push through obstacles and achieve remarkable results. This is why it gives me pause when education programs introduce leadership methodologies but sidestep the conversation about the inner resolve and tenacity required to be successful.

This is not a criticism of the institutions or instructors; most programs are superb, and their faculty brilliant. But, while they've educated many great leaders, some remarkable individuals have been able to revolutionize organizations and even entire industries without their help.

Aptitude, intellect, and formal training undeniably play a role in success. However, Angela Duckworth correctly argues in her insightful book, *Grit: The Power of Passion and Perseverance*, that they're not what sets apart the world's most successful people. Duckworth's research reveals that while they are factors, the combination of passion and perseverance, what she defines as *grit*, makes the real difference. She found that high achievers across fields endure many challenges and setbacks yet persistently demonstrate commitment and perseverance.[2]

Allow me to draw on personal experience. More than once, both on the gridiron and during my 14 years in business, I've been over-matched in talent and intellect. Yet, my ability to keep going when everyone believed there was no way forward leveled the playing field. This is not to pat myself on the back because much of this early grit was simply a byproduct of not knowing any other way. Yet, as I've grown older and wiser, I've realized that grit and excellence are insepa-rably linked.

We can learn how to build high-performing teams, inspire others, cultivate a culture of trust, and produce remarkable results. But what good does it serve if we don't have an inner resolve that propels us forward in the face of adversity? While all these are vital, they pale compared to grit's raw, transformative power. In its purest form, leader-ship hinges on knowledge and the relentless spirit to rise, irrespective of the odds.

Becoming a transformational leader is not about our past experi-ences, accolades, or rank. It's leading from where we are and inspiring others to do the same.

10

Leveraging Strengths: Leading from Your Power Zone

Strengths are not activities you're good at, they're activities that strengthen you. A strength is an activity that before you're doing it, you look forward to doing it; while you're doing it, time goes by quickly and you can concentrate; after you've done it, it seems to fulfill a need of yours.

—Marcus Buckingham

WHEN I WAS younger, I believed that doing more than everyone else gave me a competitive advantage. It all had to pay off, right? Wrong. Through experience, I realized that this mindset is severely flawed and can have detrimental consequences, such as undermining our ability to engage, effect change, develop influence, and cultivate personal growth.

Accepting this truth is incredibly challenging for leaders because we often equate doing more with making progress. As author Richard Koch explains in his groundbreaking book *The 80/20 Principle: The Secret of Achieving More with Less*:

The road to hell is paved with the pursuit of volume. Volume leads to marginal products, marginal customers, and greatly increased managerial complexity . . . . Hard work leads to low returns. Insight and doing what we want leads to high returns. . . .

Strive for excellence in [a] few things, rather than good performance in many. . . . It is not [a] shortage of time that should worry us, but the tendency for the majority of [our] time to be spent in low-quality ways. . . . The 80/20 principle says that if we doubled our time on the top 20 percent of activities, we could work a two-day week and achieve 60 percent more than [we do] now.[1]

A Skewed Metric

Nothing undermines this philosophy like the misguided premise that action equals achievement. While living by this skewed metric may satisfy the restless nature of those with big dreams and high hopes, it's a slippery slope. As previously discussed, having a leadership title does not mean you're impacting and influencing the lives of those around you; the same is true regarding how we spend our days. Just because you appear busy doesn't mean you're being productive. Unfortunately, this flawed metric traps far too many potentially outstanding leaders, severely restricting their capacity to lead and have an impact.

How often have you heard someone say that being active doesn't necessarily mean you're doing anything of substance? If you're anything like me, more than a few. Despite the widespread popularity of this adage, it's rare for individuals to step away from their daily routines long enough to question whether their actions have a purpose.

To illustrate this, I'll share a famous fable. Once, in a small village, there were two lumberjacks named Sam and Jed. Both men were competitive and decided to hold a contest to determine who could chop the most firewood in a single day. The next morning at dawn, the men began cutting on different sides of the house. While Sam could hear Jed chopping, he soon noticed something odd: Jed would stop chopping for 15 minutes every hour. Thinking this was to his advantage, Sam continued chopping without taking breaks. By the time the sun set, Sam was exhausted but confident he had won. However, to his surprise, Jed had chopped significantly more wood. Sam asked, "How did you chop more wood when I heard you take a break every hour?" Jed replied, "Those weren't breaks; I was sharpening my axe."

This story teaches us that it's not just about staying busy, but also ensuring that our actions are efficient and focused. Like Sam, many equate constant movement with productivity, but without reflection, strategy, and rest, we're working with a dull blade. To maximize productivity, we must recognize the value of adopting a strategic and contemplative mindset when navigating the complexities of leadership. This is neither a call to action nor a guarantee that being strategic will make you a transformational leader. Nevertheless, it's imperative to recognize that no matter our efforts and intentions, we undermine our potential by equating busyness with achievement. Taking the time to "sharpen your axe" will lead to far better results.

Hindered Development

A trend emerges during performance evaluations, annual reviews, and talent calibration sessions—the spotlight shifts from celebrating strengths to highlighting weaknesses. Not only does this do a disservice to the evaluated individual, but it also diminishes the productivity of the leaders engaged in the discussion. I'm not saying we should overlook weaknesses or ignore areas that demand improvement. But it begs the question: what competencies are essential for optimum performance, and how are we measuring up?

Research shows that focusing on an individual's weaknesses or continuously recognizing their shortcomings doesn't foster growth. Furthermore, when our position doesn't amplify our strengths, we're at a higher risk of mediocrity, underperformance, and feeling unfulfilled.

Case in point: an organization I advise was concerned about a high-potential leader whose performance had declined over the previous half-year. The company's CEO asked me to spend some time with the struggling leader to pinpoint the reason for his declining performance and negative attitude. Entrusted with the task, I reviewed his leadership development profile, spoke with human resources, and analyzed his past contributions. The organization's belief in the leader's potential wasn't misplaced. He was among the company's top performers in his previous position. Recognizing this, well-intentioned executives transferred him to a more pivotal role, expecting him to replicate his past success.

After several insightful meetings with him, it was clear that the heart of the problem wasn't merely trouble adjusting to his new position. The organization had overlooked what previously fueled his success. From my research and analyses, two distinct reasons stood out:

1. An exceptionally skilled leader, he thrived in roles that allowed him more involvement in the nuance of business operations. This was where he shined the brightest.
2. His ability to foster teamwork and build consensus was unmatched. The new, more client-centric role distanced him from team interactions, his driving force.

His productivity, performance, and job satisfaction suffered even with a higher salary. This was not surprising since it was clear he was intrinsically motivated. He'd accepted the new role because he wanted to be a team player and do what was best for the company. The organization failed to understand what motivated and empowered this leader.

Before our sessions, internal discussions focused on his shortcomings, inefficiencies, and weaknesses. However, after discussing his unique strengths for a couple of months, the conversation changed to how best to use his abilities in this new role. The upshot? Both his performance and fulfillment quickly increased.

The takeaway: When we operate within our power zone, we deliver our best and inspire the best in others.

Discovering Your Power Zone

If focusing on strengths rather than weaknesses drives growth and development, then a key question emerges: how can we identify our strengths and harness the influence necessary to access a plane of potential where all is possible? I call this the *power zone*. It's a mindset, a state of being, an almost Zen-like environment of consciousness where we're free to produce our best work and impact the world.

1. Harness the Power of Self-Assessment

Professional self-assessment tools are analytical in helping us identify our core strengths and capabilities. Some of the most authoritative and globally recognized tools include:

- Gallup CliftonStrengths: Renowned for identifying unique talents.[2]

- The Predictive Index: Provides insight into the capacity to learn and adapt.[3]
- Hogan Assessments: Effective in aligning personalities with professional roles.[4]
- Myers-Briggs Personality Type Indicator: Inventory to identify personality and strengths.[5]
- The Enneagram: A map of self-discovery and growth based on personality types.[6]
- Keirsey Temperament Sorter: Determines how the environment impacts productivity.[7]
- Strong Interest Inventory: Determines work personality type using interests.[8]

These assessments are multifaceted, often evaluating both personality types and individual strengths. They've been validated by decades of research, attesting to their reliability in offering actionable insights. Whether you're just starting your career path or pivoting to a new phase, leveraging these assessments can be a game-changer, arming you with the knowledge to optimize your potential and excel in your field.

2. Ask for Constructive Feedback

Many organizations embrace 360-degree feedback for their leaders and managers. While institutional assessments are insightful, I've discovered that self-initiated 360 evaluations can deliver sharper, more actionable results. Regardless of position, anyone can benefit from seeking feedback from peers. This proactive approach offers a mirror to how the world perceives us.

While it's crucial to chart our path without being unduly influenced by others' opinions, diverse perspectives can illuminate our self-awareness blind spots. This is true even for seasoned leaders; our self-image and how others perceive us can diverge significantly. Pursuing personal growth and seeking genuine feedback can inspire others to provide truthful, constructive insight. To kick-start this introspective journey, here are a few questions I've found helpful:

1. From your perspective, what are my greatest three qualities?
2. Which trait gives me the capacity to attain excellence?
3. What are three unique attributes that set me apart from others?

4. Do you think I'm leveraging my core strengths and qualities to their fullest potential?
5. Where were my top three abilities instrumental in achieving a goal?
6. If you were to recommend an area for me to develop further, what would it be?

These questions serve as foundational prompts; tailor them to align with your journey. The overarching goal is to leverage diverse perspectives for self-awareness and growth. Insights from those around us can unveil nuances about ourselves, sharpen our focus, and even identify and challenge limiting beliefs.

Consistently seeking feedback has shaped my understanding of my strengths, helping me refine my power zone and accentuate my unique value proposition. Regular self-assessments allow you to crystallize your distinctive strengths and chart a more informed path forward.

3. What Invigorates You?

When we invest time and effort into identifying and developing our strengths, it's not unusual to feel a surge of energy. Aligning with our natural talents often gives us a sense of vitality. I experience this every time I step onstage to speak. Whether it's for an audience of five business leaders or 5,000, an unparalleled sense of dynamism and renewal washes over me. How powerful is it? While football has long been my passion, the feeling of playing in front of thousands of cheering fans doesn't compare to the fulfilling thrill of sharing my message and having it resonate with audiences worldwide. This stems from a profound alignment among my words, heart, and soul.

This isn't about your weekend hobbies or favorite pastimes. It's about analyzing your daily responsibilities and pinpointing what invigorates you. If you're thinking "easier said than done," I have an exercise that may help. For the next week, carry a notebook and write down what you do daily. At the end of each day, reflect on the moments that brought you joy and note any emerging themes. After a couple of days, you'll notice a pattern that'll help connect increased energy with specific tasks and activities.

Identifying what energizes us throughout the day is a smart way to discern our strengths, helping us channel more time into our areas of excellence and operate in our power zone.

4. What Do Others Compliment?

What is your response when someone offers you a compliment? Some people respond with a simple "thank you," while others are in the habit of deflecting kind words. It's polite to thank them, but the most important thing you can do is take note. Listening to what others praise most is an effective method for identifying strengths. Each of us possesses innate talents and abilities. Other people's insights are necessary since conducting a completely objective self-assessment is impossible. Gaining a clear understanding through other people's eyes enables us to leverage our strengths and effectively boost our performance.

Like many, I grew up watching *Mister Rogers' Neighborhood*. While Fred Rogers was a trained musical composer and ordained minister, he may have never fully recognized his true strength without feedback from those around him. Early in his career, parents, educators, and peers consistently praised his ability to entertain, but more so his ability to show genuine empathy. Fred Rogers's talent was making children feel seen and heard and discussing complex issues in a way they could understand. Talk with a parent who had little ones when his show was on the air, and you'll hear how Mister Rogers's simple yet profound words helped their children navigate difficult situations like grief or bullying.

In 1981, 5-year-old Jeffrey Erlanger appeared on the show to discuss why he used a wheelchair.[9] Mister Rogers's kindness made the young guest feel comfortable, valued, and understood. The episode is a testament to Rogers's ability to connect with children on an emotional level. Tom Hanks told *Vanity Fair* Magazine that seeing Mr. Rogers interact with Erlanger is "one of the reasons I'm in the movie," referring to his Academy Award–nominated portrayal of the beloved television personality in the 2019 film *A Beautiful Day in the Neighborhood*.[10] His impact on Erlanger was so significant that 18 years later, he surprised Rogers onstage during the icon's induction into the Television Hall of

Fame. While Rogers was a talented musician, storyteller, and television host, his unparalleled empathy cemented his legacy.

Recognizing the components of ourselves that receive the most praise isn't merely an exercise in self-affirmation. For figures like Fred Rogers, it became a compass guiding their contributions to society. Such awareness can empower individuals to elevate their performance, providing an unmatched professional edge. Remember to listen the next time you receive a compliment; the other person may see something you missed.

5. Be Open to the Unfamiliar

In our personal and professional lives, we often limit our potential by playing it safe and sticking to what we know. Many of us tread familiar paths, fearing the unknown or the unpredictable. However, a life lived within the confines of the familiar can prevent us from discovering our true strengths, passions, and areas of excellence—our power zones. Here are some more advantages of breaking free from the monotony of sameness:

- **Broadens Your Skill Set:** Trying new things equips you with new skills. For example, suppose you've always run team meetings a certain way, but you take a course on boosting team productivity. In that case, you may discover a new tactic for more effective meetings, a new approach that could change everything about how you connect.
- **Enhances Adaptability:** Openness to new experiences trains the brain to adapt to unforeseen circumstances. This adaptability is a personal and professional strength, allowing you to handle challenges with resilience and flexibility.
- **Builds Confidence:** Stepping out of your comfort zone and succeeding (or even failing and learning from it) can drastically boost your self-confidence. Over time, you'll develop a belief in your ability to handle diverse situations, making you more assertive and decisive.

- **Promotes Interdisciplinary Thinking:** The most revolutionary innovations often occur at the intersection of disciplines. Being open to diverse experiences can give you a broad perspective, enabling you to connect seemingly unrelated dots and develop unique solutions.

While comfort zones have their allure, they often become barriers to discovering profound potential. Every fresh challenge or new situation is an opportunity for growth. So, let's not rest on the familiar but dare to be uncomfortable; only then can we thrive in our power zone.

11

Leading with Strengths: How the Best Get Even Better

The great leaders are like the best conductors, they reach beyond the notes to reach the magic in the players.

—Blaine Lee

BILL BELICHICK. You don't have to be from Boston or count yourself among the 16.7 million football fans[1] who watch the NFL each Sunday to recognize his name. If you're drawing a blank, ask the person next to you; someone will know. How can I be so sure? Since becoming the head coach of the New England Patriots in 2000, Belichick has led his team to accumulate 17 AFC East division titles and six Super Bowl rings.[2] When the 3× Coach of the Year finally hangs up his well-worn gray sweatshirt and retires, the Pro Football Hall of Fame will be waiting with open arms to immortalize his outstanding career. Why? He's arguably one of the greatest coaches in the history of professional sports.

Several things may come to mind when I mention Belichick's name. Perhaps it's New England's dominance with the legendary Tom Brady at the helm, those Super Bowls where a Patriots victory seemed a foregone conclusion, or those now-famous press conferences where Belichick's one-word responses kept it brief.

What strikes me is his ability to get the most out of his players, quarter after quarter, game after game, and season after season. This is only possible because of his ability to identify a player's potential and position them to do their best. It's why the Patriots have had a knack for reviving the careers of players other teams write off and helping overlooked rookies find their groove. Consider that seemingly risky sixth-round draft pick that so-called experts predicted would never succeed in the league. New England set him up for success and handed him the ball—now he's a household name.

When asked what he's learned most from Coach Belichick, Assistant Head Coach Joe Judge explained, "To be flexible with your personnel. Don't try to shove round pegs into square holes. Figure out what you have. Let them play to their strengths. Don't sit in a meeting and tell me what you don't have in a player; don't tell me they can't do a certain thing."[3]

Belichick's ability to capitalize on his players' strengths and exploit them for the team's benefit is one of the many reasons for his success. While the Super Bowl victories, the records, and the dynasty he established are what people obsess over, these are just byproducts of an organization that excels at strengths-based leadership.

Strengths-Based Leadership: The Underlying Principle

In 2009, a team of experts from Gallup set out to answer the seminal question of our time: what makes an effective leader? This meant sorting through 50 years of polling, 20,000 interviews, and studies on more than a million teams worldwide. After this extensive undertaking, team members Tom Rath and Barry Conchie published their findings in *Strengths-Based Leadership: Great Leaders, Teams, and Why People Follow*. The authors argue that there isn't a single definitive list of traits that make a great leader. Instead, the most influential leaders know their strengths and weaknesses and surround themselves with people who complement and counterbalance those. Through this lens, great leaders focus on building what's strong rather than fixing what's wrong.[4]

The Secret Sauce of Successful Leaders

Chapter 10 focused on the critical importance of leaders discovering their strengths and leading from their power zone. But what's the impact of leaders placing team members in positions that maximize their strengths? We're in good shape if it's even a quarter of Coach Belichick's.

Imagine two groups of workers—one buzzing enthusiastically, the other counting the clock. What separates the two? Gallup dug into this question with two compelling studies, one before and one after the pandemic. They found it's all about where you pour your time and energy. The happier, more engaged employees spent up to five times more time developing and leveraging their strengths. In contrast, the dissatisfied employees squandered their days by splitting time between strengths and weaknesses. That's the equivalent of a master chef dividing his time equally between the kitchen and the janitorial closet.[5]

I know what you're thinking: "Does this mean we ignore our flaws and just wing it?" Absolutely not! Authentic engagement means adopting a strengths-first philosophy and doing more of what makes you extraordinary. Allocate your time wisely; invest more in what you, or your teammates, do spectacularly well.[6]

What do you get when you focus on strengths? Energy. We're talking about an energy that seems to come from nowhere and bursts of innovation and creativity that would've made Steve Jobs do a double take. Does this sound too good to be true? Here's the data to back it up: organizations that integrate a "strengths-centric" model report a staggering 19% jump in sales, a 25% boost in profits, and a 5% hike in customer satisfaction.[7]

When Howard Schultz returned to Starbucks as CEO in 2008, the company was in a crisis, suffering from a poor economy and increased competition. Schultz immediately took action to turn around the company; one of his most important decisions was recognizing and utilizing his team's strengths.

Schultz understood the importance of putting people in roles aligned with their strengths. He also ensured managers received leadership training, enabling them to motivate their teams and bring out the best in each employee. Instead of telling customer service personnel to be polite, the company trained and encouraged them to go above and beyond to make the customer's experience memorable. These roles played to the employees' core strengths.

During this time, Schultz made another crucial decision: he chose not to focus on weaknesses but on what his team did best. Not only did

Starbucks survive the financial crisis, but it emerged more vital than ever. By 2013, Starbucks's stock price had tripled, customer satisfaction was higher than ever, and employees, from baristas to managers, were more engaged because they were positioned to excel.[8]

Starbucks is an example of what happens when leaders understand the value of focusing on strengths. Schultz didn't just improve Starbucks; he transformed it into a more resilient, profitable, and beloved brand. He knew the incredible impact of putting people in positions that maximized their strengths. Let's face it: whether you're an intern or CEO, who wouldn't want to be part of a workplace where people are not simply counting down the hours but making the hours count?

Positive Psychology: The Science of Strength

The leadership playbook has shifted. It's no longer about earning titles and boosting quarterly reports; it has become an art form that elicits efficiency and brilliance. Still, misconceptions and out-of-date mindsets exist surrounding strengths-based leadership. I recently discussed this philosophy with an insurance executive, who told me that a worker's affinity for a role is irrelevant. "Hey, they took the job," he explained. "If they perform, maybe they get promoted to a position where they can utilize their strengths," he added.

That's the real treat—a position that aligns with one's strengths is a reward for succeeding in a less-fitting role. Such thinking runs counter to the thesis of strengths-based leadership. While identifying and magnifying strengths may initially demand extra time and energy, it's a price that transformational leaders like Coach Belichick willingly pay. Why? Because they understand that this is not just about personal satisfaction; it's the key to unlocking world-class performance and transformative impact.

Enter positive psychology, a subfield that has gained inroads into everything from education to corporate America. Unlike traditional psychological approaches that center on mental illness or dysfunction, positive psychology focuses on emotions, strengths, and well-being. Developed in the late 1990s by Martin Seligman, former President of the American Psychological Society, positive psychology provides valuable insight into how individuals and communities thrive.[9] While Seligman is often called the "Father of Positive Psychology," the contributions of Abraham Maslow are equally important, if not more so.[10]

Although the formalized field emerged decades after his death, Maslow coined the term *positive psychology* in his 1954 book *Motivation and Personality*. In addition, his ideas served as a philosophical foundation on which Seligman's team constructed their research. "The recent positive psychology movement focuses on themes addressed by Maslow over 50 years ago," explained famed humanistic psychologist Nelson Goud.[11] One of the most influential psychologists of the 20th century, Maslow is most famous for his hierarchy of needs model, which conceptualizes human needs in a pyramid structure, with physiological needs at the base and self-actualization at the peak. Maslow was interested in human potential and what constitutes psychological health. He believed that every person has an innate drive toward self-actualization—in other words, to become their best possible selves.

Maslow eventually turned his attention to the theory that individuals can only reach their peak potential when engaged in work they excel at, enjoy, and deem meaningful. He discovered that the right organization or community could have an even more profound impact on an individual than years of therapy. After all, it's not just about having a job; it's about having a calling. By emphasizing the positive aspects of human experience and the potential for growth and self-improvement, Maslow's work continues to be relevant, enriching our understanding of well-being and achievement.[12]

This isn't simply about worker satisfaction or improving the bottom line. It's a radical reimagining of what makes us function at our best. It's not about elevating just yourself but also the collective. Leading with strengths and encouragement ripples through an organization while amplifying fulfillment, satisfaction, and engagement. These aren't simply pleasant side effects; they are the fuel that powers the engine of transformational change.

If you're a leader aiming to make a lasting impact, then identifying, developing, and leveraging the strengths of others isn't just nice to have; it's non-negotiable. Welcome to transformational leadership, where helping individuals perform at their peak isn't just the right thing to do; it's the only thing to do.

Strengths-Based Leadership in Action

This chapter discussed several principles, but three are particularly important. To bring these three to life, let's delve into the captivating true story of the 1980 U.S. Olympic ice hockey team, commonly known as the "Miracle on Ice." Far from a corporate boardroom or tech startup, the team was a ragtag group of amateur players led by Coach Herb Brooks.[13]

1. **Discover your unique strengths and operate from your power zone:** Coach Brooks didn't have the most technically skilled team and knew he couldn't compete head-on with a Soviet team that had taken gold in four straight Olympic Games. But he understood that his strength as a coach was forging a team greater than the sum of its parts. He operated from this power zone, focusing on relentless training, mental preparation, and team unity.

2. **Be the catalyst for others to discover their strengths:** Brooks didn't attempt to make his team something they weren't. Instead, he helped them find their unique strengths, such as being younger, faster, and suited for a more grueling pace. He reshaped their gameplay to exploit these assets.

3. **Look for the untapped potential in others and help them access it:** The coach saw potential, whereas others saw inexperience. He didn't focus on what his players lacked regarding world-stage experience; he put his energy into surprising the other team with untapped speed, grit, and physicality.

By applying these principles, the team achieved the impossible by defeating the heavily favored Soviet Union in a historic 4–3 upset. Two days later, Team USA won gold by defeating Finland. Even more remarkable is how these young men grew under Brooks's leadership. While more than half of these players went on to have successful careers in the NHL, all had the transformative experience of playing under a leader who could identify, leverage, and harness their strengths.

Strengths-based leadership isn't merely a tool for professional development; it's a philosophy that can revolutionize your impact. Imagine the transformative effect you can have on your child by teaching them not to march through life but to dance through it with a sense of self-awareness and curiosity. Picture a partnership or marriage, not as a compromise but as a symphony of two individuals contributing their best selves—distinct notes creating a melody.

Transformational leadership isn't a position; it's a creed. It demands the relentless pursuit of excellence and an unwavering commitment to lift others, helping them use their unique strengths as the bedrock for building a better world. Is that why many "leadership" positions fail? Partially, it also stems from the harsh reality that dissatisfaction, diminished self-confidence, and unfulfilled aspirations emanate from an obsessive focus on what's missing or flawed within us. This culture of deficiency and numbness bleeds into our leadership styles, blinding us to the individual brilliance of those we're meant to inspire. Instead of focusing on their flaws, Coach Brooks highlighted player strengths and fostered an environment where they could shine. When we evaluate, mentor, or coach through a diminished lens, choosing to see what people lack, we become architects of mediocrity rather than engineers of excellence.

While we should not forget that weakness requires attention, we should devote most of our energy to remembering that strengths are the key to transformative change. The genius behind Herb Brooks, Bill Belichick, and others like them is that they understand the significance of leveraging what's already extraordinary within us and those we lead. It's not about mitigating weakness but amplifying strengths to a volume that drowns out shortcomings. There, we uncover boundless possibilities and lay the cornerstone for a brighter future.

When you adopt this leadership style, you write a story that, like the Miracle on Ice, stands as an enduring testament to the potential within each of us.

12

Engaging Hearts and Minds: Beyond Talents and Tactics

Engaging the hearts, minds, and hands of talent is the most sustainable source of competitive advantage.

—Greg Harris

WHAT SETS WINNING teams apart from those that seemingly have it all yet crumble under pressure? Why do some transcend limitations, rise above roadblocks, and succeed against significantly more talented competitors? This question has always captivated, fascinated, and compelled me. However, before I reveal what I believe to be the magic ingredient, let's address the usual suspects—those factors that, while important, don't guarantee success:

- Individual talent.
- Brilliant strategy.
- Clear communication.
- Hard work.
- Skill diversity.
- Regular training.
- Decades of experience.
- Effective tools and platforms.

- Strong management.
- Unlimited resources.

You may think, "Aren't these the hallmarks of excellence?" While they're pivotal components of a winning team and crucial for consistent success, each is merely a piece of the puzzle, not the complete picture.

Consider this: if sheer talent were the key, teams with incredibly talented individuals would never fail. Yet history is full of extraordinary talents who fail to leave their mark. While they certainly left a mark, a story that comes to mind is that of the 1992 U.S. Olympic basketball team—the illustrious "Dream Team." With basketball legends like Michael Jordan, Charles Barkley, Scottie Pippen, Larry Bird, and Magic Johnson, the team was unbeatable—on paper. Yet, as they prepared for the world stage, they suffered a humbling defeat to a team of top NCAA players. This 20-minute scrimmage in San Diego, California, was not just a loss but a humiliating experience for some of the greatest players in history. Pippen reflected on this shocking upset, saying, "These young kids were killing us. We didn't know how to play with each other."

This isn't just an anecdote. It's a revelation. While important, raw talent alone is not the key to victory. The real magic lies in unity, in the ability of individuals to sync their rhythms and complement each other's abilities. After the loss, Michael Jordan told the Los Angeles Times, "We got killed today. They beat us and played well. We're out of sync and unsure about things we're [normally] comfortable with."[1] The next day, the teams faced off again. When discussing the rematch, Grant Hill, who played on the NCAA team and went on to play in the NBA, said, "We couldn't get the ball over half-court." A motivated Dream Team had found their rhythm, beat the college players by over 100 points, and swept through the 1992 Summer Olympic Games undefeated to win gold. Having great players is one thing; getting them to play as a single, effective unit is another. And that is where the heart of victory resides.[2]

Why Hearts and Minds?

Deeply rooted in military strategy, "winning hearts and minds" signifies the importance of fostering trust, unity, and mutual understanding.

Emanating from Britain's effort during the Malayan Emergency in the late 1940s and 1950s, the concept signified the importance of winning the support and trust of the local population as part of an overarching strategic goal that included tactical success.[3]

While applied in a very different context, the underlying principle remains the same: victory doesn't only depend on superior firepower (talent), but also on deeper, intangible factors such as understanding, cohesion, and trust. Just as a military force needs the local populace on its side, teams require shared knowledge and mutual trust to rise above challenges and succeed.

The 1992 Dream Team had the firepower, but raw talent wasn't enough. It wasn't until they engaged their hearts and minds and achieved a shared purpose that they were free to dominate. Whether it's the battlefield, basketball court, or boardroom, we must win hearts and minds to achieve greatness.

Lessons from a Hall of Fame Coach

In exploring what distinguishes extraordinary teams from the rest, let's stay with professional basketball a bit longer and look at the San Antonio Spurs. It's easy to look at numbers—the victories, the championships—and believe they tell the whole story. But peel back a layer, and there's more to discover.

The Spurs are, without question, one of the most successful franchises in recent decades. Not just in basketball but in any sport. Their consistent achievements result from a leadership style emphasizing human connection; the team's head coach, Gregg Popovich, is often praised for genuinely caring for his players.

Tales of Popovich's invitation-only dinners, where basketball takes a backseat to discussions about life, current events, and wine, are as legendary as the team's five NBA Championships under his leadership. Former Spurs' guard Danny Green says, "The dinners help us better understand each [other], which brings us closer [together]." This off-court investment in understanding and guiding his players makes Popovich's approach stand out. Former San Antonio center Pau Gasol explains, "I haven't been a part of this anywhere else. And players know the importance of it . . . and how important it is to Pop."[4]

Think back to our earlier discussion about the essence of top-tier teams. I emphasized the importance of cohesion and unity. Popovich, in many ways, serves as a case study. While his coaching brilliance is unquestionable, his dedication to the holistic development of his players has cemented his legacy.

By now, you might see where I'm going with this. The San Antonio Spurs' success is rooted in more than individual talent, brilliant strategy, hard work, diverse skills, regular training, experience, and unlimited resources; it reflects a leadership philosophy that moves beyond directives and drills. Instead, Popovich engages the hearts and minds of individuals, blending them into a cohesive, potent unit. It's a lesson in leadership that transcends sports, underscoring the importance of connection, understanding, and mutual respect.

Becoming a Humble Servant

Having people listen to you because you're their boss isn't the same as effectively engaging their hearts and minds. Leaders who issue orders may help organizations hit targets and enjoy limited success, but that's far from igniting that spark of excellence that fosters transformation. Achievement isn't just about task completion or meeting benchmarks. While operating at par may occasionally deliver favorable outcomes, profound change occurs when we resonate with those we lead, tapping into their aspirations and motivations.

At the center of transformative leadership stands the servant leader. Far removed from expecting privilege due to rank, they flip the script entirely. Their philosophy? Service above self. They see themselves not as commanders but as advocates, consistently putting the needs of others before their own. Transformational leaders embody a mindset of working on behalf of others. Reed Hastings, the founder of Netflix, has been successful by any standard. During his early days as an engineer, before Netflix, he was somewhat of a workaholic, arriving at the office before dawn, leaving late in the evening, and leaving a trail of used coffee mugs in his wake.

Like clockwork, those mugs would be cleaned and placed on his desk weekly. Reed naturally attributed this to the janitorial staff. Yet, one morning, he found the company's CEO washing those mugs.

He asked the CEO why he had washed the mugs. The CEO responded, "You do so much for us; this is the least I can do for you." That single act of humility, performed without any desire for credit, cemented Reed's respect and loyalty. He wasn't just working for a CEO; he was a true leader. He was inspired, and he said he would follow that leader anywhere.[5] Such stories remind us that genuine, often understated acts make the greatest impact.

PART

IV

Undergoing a Personal Metamorphosis

13

Becoming More: The Intersection of Potential and Transformation

The journey of a thousand miles begins with a single step.

—Lao Tzu

FOR ME, THAT single step was a lesson learned after an intense Sunday morning speed training session. I was a junior in high school and had just set a new personal best in the 40-yard dash. I felt invincible. Standing beside me was my very first coach—my father. In my first book, *Winning Plays*, I discuss my high school years in more detail. If you haven't read it, know that those years revolved around my football career and pushing myself.

I was proud of what I'd achieved, and for good reason. At home, I had a stack of recruitment letters from some of the top college football programs in the country, proof that my hard work was paying off. As we returned to the car, my father said something that shaped my worldview and put me on the path to lasting success. Although he was a man of few words, when he spoke, you listened. "Matt, you have potential, and I'm proud of you," he said, looking me in the eye, "But remember, the world is full of people with potential. It's not about having it; it's about what you do with it. The question isn't whether you can play football; it's whether you're willing to do what it takes to succeed."

That was a wake-up call. For far too long, I'd coasted on coaches telling me my potential would carry me through. My father's job was to prepare me for reality, and the truth was that relying on potential and talent was dangerous and reckless. Later that evening, he explained that many talented athletes fail to advance to the next level; some hang out with the wrong crowd, others don't take their academics seriously, and many rely on their natural athleticism and talent alone.

Potential: The Double-Edged Sword

You've got a gift—something that can change lives. This isn't to pump you full of empty slogans and motivational nonsense, but to help you pursue excellence. The wisdom my father imparted on me that crisp Sunday morning also applies to you. So, recognize that natural talent is your first step, not the entire journey. We all have the raw materials—the talent, intelligence, and charisma—needed to shape our destiny. Some of us may have a head start, but that initial advantage does not guarantee success.

How often have you heard someone say, "That person has potential"? I hear it constantly, especially from executives eyeing their organization's next generation of leaders. Like an ever-present cloud, potential can hover over our heads for years, becoming less of an accolade and more of an albatross. I've met countless leaders with incredible potential who never rise and advance; they get eclipsed by someone with less talent who hustles, prioritizes, and gets things done.

We must understand that there's a delicate balance between innate talent and the grit required to convert potential into reality. There will always be those for whom it comes easy; the thing is, they're outliers. I've seen ordinary people, including plenty of transformational leaders, achieve extraordinary things through commitment, determination, and effort. So, don't rely on talent alone; set yourself apart by being disciplined, dedicated, and relentless.

The Five Core Tenets of Effective Leadership

With an abundance of leadership development resources ranging from books and articles to online courses and academic programs, the journey to becoming an impactful leader can be fantastic one moment and overwhelming the next. With so much great information, it may feel like the universe is raining golden opportunities. Are you catching the droplets or just getting wet?

That depends on whether you're climbing the corporate ladder, navigating the nuances of a startup, coaching a sports team, or using your leadership abilities for something entirely different. Why? Because the leadership playbook differs depending on what you're striving to achieve. Becoming a better leader is just one piece of a complex puzzle. You may be great at your job and enjoy crushing deadlines, but you have work to do if your team resembles a flock of lost sheep. The same is true if your talented team operates in a silo, cut off from the rest of the organization.

While the path to effective leadership is not one-size-fits-all, these five core tenets are universal:

1. Self-leadership.
2. People leadership.
3. Team leadership.
4. Organizational leadership.
5. Transitional leadership.

1. Self-Leadership: Being Your Own North Star

In Chapters 7 and 8, we ventured beyond the superficial to explore a profound truth: internal quality is the blueprint for external impact. Yet that scratches the surface of a more multidimensional concept.

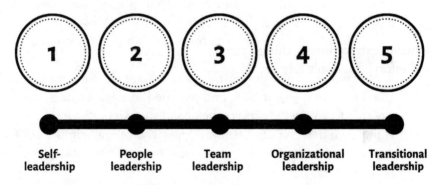

Figure 13.1   Five Core Tenets of Effective Leadership.

To underscore the importance of self-leadership, let's look at Aron Ralston, an adventurer whose story became the basis for the 2010 movie *127 Hours*.[1] James Franco portrayed Ralston in the film, for which he received his first and only Academy Award nomination.

In 2003, Aron Ralston went hiking alone in Utah's remote Canyonlands National Park. Unfortunately, he became trapped in a narrow slot canyon when a boulder fell and pinned his arm. For six days, Ralston remained trapped, rationing a small amount of food and water while attempting to free himself. Ultimately, he faced a horrific decision: amputate his arm or perish.[2]

Let's explore how Ralston's decisions during this stressful, high-stakes ordeal match up against the principles of self-leadership:

- **Unwavering Integrity:** In a world hooked on social approval, having the courage to adhere to your values, even when no one is watching, speaks volumes. It's not about the applause; it's about staying true to your moral compass and ensuring it points north. Facing the possibility of death, Ralston recorded brutally honest video messages for his family. He was transparent about the mistakes that led him to that situation, including not telling anyone his whereabouts.
- **Insatiable Curiosity:** A relentless drive to evolve, challenge the status quo, and reach beyond our comfort zone promotes continuous growth. Even in such dire straits, Ralston used his engineering background to construct a makeshift pulley system to lift the boulder.
- **Proactive Excellence:** Be the pacesetter, not the pacekeeper. In other words, set the standard rather than waiting for others to act. When he realized the pulley was insufficient, Ralston never stopped looking for a way out. Instead of waiting to be rescued, he took fate into his own hands.
- **Unbreakable Commitment:** In a world of fleeting interests, transactional relationships, and penciled-in engagements, staying true to your word sets you head and shoulders above the rest. Ralston didn't give up on life despite the overwhelming odds against him. He committed himself to surviving and proved successful.

- **Emotional Agility:** Stress is inevitable, but how you navigate it is optional. Develop coping mechanisms that transform stress into a springboard for growth. Through it all, Ralston displayed remarkable emotional resilience. Recognizing the situation's weight, he used the camera's remaining power to record farewell videos for his family. Still, he never allowed stress or emotions to stop him from focusing on his primary objective: survival.
- **Habitual Mastery:** Forget fads and flash-in-the-pan techniques. Adopt healthy routines and build sustainable habits that enhance performance rather than hinder it. Ralston's prior outdoor experience and engineering background enabled him to endure this ordeal and free himself.

Mastering self-leadership allowed Ralston to survive and transform his life. Post-incident, he became an inspirational speaker and wilderness safety advocate. If an individual trapped in a slot canyon can demonstrate such exceptional self-leadership, imagine what we can accomplish in our resource-rich environment.

Let me ask a blunt question: how can someone lead others if they can't lead themselves? Still, people attempt it, often resulting in ruined reputations, rash decisions, and receding victories. It amazes me how many people strategize their way up the career ladder without mastering the most crucial rung. After all, self-leadership is not some bullet point on a resume or box to check; it's the powerful undercurrent that flows through all other forms of leadership.

2. People Leadership: Influencing Individual Growth

So, you've mastered self-leadership—the art of motivating, developing, and caring for yourself. What's next? The next level isn't a title, promotion, or notch on the career ladder. No, it's something far more significant: leading others. This isn't about getting people to follow you because their job depends on it; it's about becoming someone they want to follow.

We've touched on this before—the modern dilemma of self-centered leadership. Despite what pundits tell us, authentic leadership is absent in the lecture halls of our most prestigious universities, the boardrooms of Wall Street, and beneath the magnificent white dome of the U.S. Capitol. We live in a world where it's too easy to get caught up in the "me, myself, and I" narrative. Although many leaders are obsessed with their goals, ambitions, and metrics, we must never forget that leadership is not about the journey of one but the voyage of many. Want to resonate as a phenomenal leader? Live by these three principles:

- **Put People First:** This isn't about being liked but valuing those you lead. This means understanding their aspirations, recognizing their challenges, and appreciating them as individuals. When people feel seen and valued, they don't just work for you; they work with you.
- **Be a Believer:** As a leader, you're uniquely positioned to act as a catalyst for change and growth in others. When you believe in people and see the best in them, you ignite a spark that can set off a chain reaction of self-belief and achievement. You aren't just managing people; you're transforming lives.
- **Cultivate Mutual Growth:** Remember, leadership isn't a zero-sum game where one person's gain is another's loss. You aren't detracting from your worth when you help others grow— whether in skills, confidence, or visibility—you're amplifying it.

You never know what will happen when you lead people according to these three principles. Mr. Harrison was a high school history teacher. He held no notable titles, no advanced degrees, and wasn't particularly charismatic. Yet, when you walked into his classroom, you felt like you had entered a different world. He greeted each student by name, and it was clear he knew their strengths and challenges.

One student, Emily, was struggling academically and socially. The consensus among faculty was that she was an underperformer who wouldn't go far. However, Mr. Harrison believed she had untapped potential; more importantly, he told her that. He took the time to mentor her, often staying late to help her understand the material and encouraging her to participate in class discussions. As the weeks passed, Emily started to believe in herself. As her grades improved, she became more confident and engaged. By the end of the school year, she had become an excellent student who took it upon herself to mentor other struggling students.

Years later, Emily received a full academic scholarship to college and eventually started a community organization mentoring at-risk youth. When asked about her transformation, she said, "It all started with Mr. Harrison believing in me when no one else did." Mr. Harrison epitomizes what it means to be a transformational leader. He valued his students, believed in their inherent potential, and understood that helping others would make his life more meaningful.

Leadership is not an occupation; it's a calling. It's not about climbing ladders; it's about building bridges. The world may be changing, but one thing that never will is the need for genuine, caring people. Impactful leaders understand that life's most significant rewards are the meaningful connections they forge and the lives they touch.

3. Team Leadership: Beyond the Sum of Its Parts

Effective team leadership is a complex blend of competencies, soft skills, and strategies—not authoritative control or charismatic influence. Often, when someone struggles to be a strong leader, they haven't invested the time and energy into getting to know the people they lead. Inspiring team excellence requires that a leader be familiar with each member's background, experiences, and values. If you want to become a more capable team leader, act from the standpoint of:

- **Team Excellence Is Superior:** The first principle recognizes the value of individual contributions but elevates collective achievement. Exceptional individual talent becomes exponentially more valuable when serving a common purpose. A team leader who grasps this can create an environment in which individuals work together toward a collective goal. This involves recognizing these talents and allocating them in a manner that best serves the team's objectives. It's not just about being a star player but enhancing each other's abilities and covering each other's weaknesses.
- **Greater than the Sum of Its Parts:** This principle reflects the idea of synergy. When people collaborate effectively, they

produce a far more significant outcome than they ever could working separately. For this to happen, a team leader must instill a culture of collaboration, mutual respect, and open communication. This culture is the lifeblood of rapid problem-solving and efficient execution, where intimate knowledge of each team member's skills becomes invaluable, and combining unique perspectives in pursuit of innovative solutions makes all the difference.

- **Never Tolerate Undermining Behaviors:** The third principle is critical for maintaining the integrity and productivity of a team. In any group, the possibility of interpersonal conflicts and divisive behavior exists. These could be overt, such as bullying or scapegoating, or more subtle, like cliques or passive aggressiveness. An effective leader must possess the emotional intelligence to identify such behaviors early on and the courage to address them in real time. Ignoring or tolerating these issues can damage team cohesion and undermine its members' performance and psychological safety.

- **Transcend Transactional Relationships:** Leadership must be more than transactional; exchanging pleasantries and providing selective assistance won't cut it. It's about establishing authentic relationships. This involves understanding who your team members are and what drives, challenges, and inspires them. Building these relationships can take time, but they're essential for building trust, which is the foundation of effective teamwork.

- **Growth Through Ideas and Insights:** Team leadership is not static; it requires continuous growth, adaptation, and learning. An effective team leader should act as a catalyst for group thought and discussion. They should continually encourage the team to push boundaries, be creative, and think critically. This involves more than introducing new strategies or procedures. It includes fostering an atmosphere of continuous improvement where every member feels comfortable sharing ideas and critiques openly.

Exceptional team leadership is multidimensional and requires a nuanced approach that blends emotional intelligence, strategic thinking, and authentic relationship-building. These qualities enable a leader to achieve team excellence and cultivate a culture of continual growth and collaboration.

4. Organizational Leadership: Cultivating a Thriving Ecosystem

Leadership is often associated with high-ranking positions like CEO, president, and head coach. Traditional thinking is that these individuals hold the reins of power and singularly influence the direction of their organizations or teams. While it's true that these roles come with broader influence and greater responsibility, leadership is not reserved for the corner office or executive suite.

Leadership potential exists throughout an organization, from the newest recruit to the seasoned veteran. That's because leadership isn't about wielding authority; it's about inspiring, making impactful contributions, and exemplifying core values. A mid-level manager who fosters a culture of openness and collaboration is exercising leadership. Similarly, a junior team member who takes the initiative to solve problems or develop innovative solutions demonstrates leadership. A leader's main objective should never be climbing to the highest rung of organizational power; while career advancement is a legitimate aspiration, it's not the benchmark of a great leader.

Impactful and transformational leadership is about adding value, whether that means enhancing productivity, contributing to team morale, or helping realize the organization's vision. Every action that pushes the team toward its goals is a form of leadership. You can still have a meaningful impact even if you never hold a traditional leadership position.

Let's delve into the core principles that guide this form of leadership:

- **Consider the Greater Good:** The first principle underscores the ethics and responsibilities of leadership. It brings an element of mindfulness to every decision and action, urging us to consider the broader implications and long-term consequences. Leaders don't act in a vacuum; every decision ripples through the organization, affecting people, projects, and performance. Operating with the greater good in mind ensures that these effects are constructive rather than detrimental. It's not only about what you do but also what you choose not to do. Inactivity creates bottlenecks, fosters confusion, or dilutes the team's efforts. Thus, this principle isn't just about avoiding harm; it's about promoting well-being and productivity throughout the organization.

- **Add Cascading Value:** Leadership doesn't end when you've checked off all your boxes for the day. True leaders look beyond their assigned responsibilities to find additional ways to create value. Cascading value means your contributions shouldn't remain at the level they were initially; they should flow down and out, benefiting others in their wake. It could be as simple as helping a struggling colleague, even if their tasks don't directly relate to yours. It could involve thinking creatively about improving an existing system, process, or workflow that makes everyone's work easier and more effective. When individuals continuously seek to add value, it creates a culture of generosity, collaboration, and continuous improvement that lifts the entire organization.

- **Think Quality, Not Quantity:** You may be tired of hearing this, but leadership is not about positional authority or the scale of your impact. So, what's it about, then? Simple: the quality of your impact, as measured through the lens of daily interactions. Are you a source of positivity? Do you encourage open dialogue? Are you empathetic to the struggles of others? The most potent form of leadership often resides in these seemingly small gestures, for they have the power to influence the atmosphere and culture of a workspace.

- **Effect Change Beyond Your Sphere:** What separates transformational leaders is their ability to effect change beyond their immediate sphere of influence. Whether you're CEO, a mid-level manager, or a junior employee, it's about looking beyond your scope to influence broader organizational outcomes. Transformational leaders view themselves as integral parts of the puzzle; they understand that their actions can impair or enhance the bigger picture.

Excelling in organizational leadership is less about your title than your daily interactions. Focusing on adding value creates fertile ground for leadership to thrive. It turns the spotlight on continual growth, encourages the sharing of ideas, and fosters an environment where individuals feel empowered to act. When people at all levels engage and contribute, the organization becomes more agile, innovative, and better suited to meet modern challenges. By shifting our perspective to see leadership as adding value daily, we open ourselves to the possibilities of making positive change and progress at any level.

5. Transitional Leadership: Guiding Through Uncertainty

Although the ability to lead through times of change and perform under pressure are crucial aspects of leadership, we rarely make them the central focus of our lives—much to our detriment. Today, change is not just inevitable but constant. Whether technological advancements, shifting market dynamics, or global crises, our personal and professional realities continually evolve. While change is disruptive and often demands swift adaptation, accepting it as a constant variable can help you:

- **Be Agile and Flexible:** In a quickly changing world, agility and flexibility become more than desirable; they become necessary. These aren't just large, visible changes but also subtle shifts that have a cumulative effect over time. If you can't guide your team through minor adjustments, how will you navigate the complexities of a significant strategic pivot or market upheaval? In the face of change, leadership is about being proactive and responsive—anticipating it where possible but also being prepared to adapt when unexpected challenges arise.
- **Strengthen Your Emotional Intelligence:** How can we develop the ability to thrive under pressure? This is where strong emotional intelligence—the ability to understand and manage your emotions and those of the people around you—becomes an asset. Under extreme stress, your decision-making, communication, and interpersonal skills break down unless you've prepared by training your emotional responses. Leaders with high emotional intelligence keep their composure and think clearly, even when the stakes are high, thereby earning the trust and confidence of their team.

■ **Be the Anchor:** Change creates uncertainty and anxiety in teams and organizations. While you may not have control over the change, you can control your verbal and nonverbal responses. While straightforward and transparent communication can help mitigate fear, projecting confidence can provide the reassurance your team needs to find a foothold. Change leadership requires emotional stability, consistency, compassion, and honesty.

Grit and Grace: The Lasting Legacy of a Leader

In a world where change is the only constant, our effectiveness in navigating and leading through change defines us. Many possess the talent and potential to become transformative leaders, but as my father explained, their potential is just the beginning; it's what they do with it that counts.

Think of your potential as a garden. To cultivate anything worthwhile, you must nurture the soil (effort) and ensure it receives adequate sunlight (discipline). Soon, the seeds of greatness that lay dormant deep inside will sprout. This growth potential is universal, whether you're navigating a life-changing hardship like Aron Ralston did in that canyon or shaping young minds in a classroom like Mr. Harrison. Leadership is fundamentally about making choices and acting, regardless of your circumstances.

So, what will you do with your potential? Allow it to remain dormant, or cultivate it for the greater good? Don't be satisfied with simply dreaming; focus on becoming and doing. The true measure of a leader is their ability to turn potential into impact. While many have potential, only a dedicated few will ever harness it. This is what separates true leaders from the rest.

Being a transformational leader is more than a role; it's an intrinsic part of your identity. As you progress, remember two things. First, this calling is not about achieving personal greatness but inspiring others to reach their full potential. Second, let grit and grace define your leadership brand; you will undoubtedly make a lasting impact.

14

Battling Self-Limiting Beliefs and Embracing Change

It's not the strongest or most intelligent who will survive but those who can best manage change.

—Charles Darwin

ELLA WAS A naturally gifted pianist; from a young age, she could perform complex pieces and was passionate about music. Unlike her peers, the 25-year-old didn't strive to be world-renowned. Instead, she dreamed of one day leading a symphony and worked tirelessly to make it a reality. After a decade of hard work, Ella felt that doors were beginning to open.

Soon after her 35th birthday, Ella became pregnant; nine months later, she was a mother. While everyone told her it would be the greatest moment of her life, she struggled with the transition. By age 45, she felt overwhelmed with immense personal and professional dissatisfaction. Instead of enjoying life's milestones, she found balancing her child's needs, caring for her aging parents, and holding on to her dreams exhausting.

When things were going well, Ella was happy and brightened every room she entered. But when she faced challenges, her mood shifted dramatically. She became increasingly focused on the negatives, often complaining about past performances and missed opportunities.

Before long, Ella had adopted a dangerous and destructive mindset: that of a victim. She saw everyone and everything as trying to prevent her from achieving her professional goals. Not only did this affect her music, but it also strained her relationships.

Family and friends eventually talked her into seeking professional help. However, her mood and outlook hadn't improved after several therapists and various medications. One therapist told her, "Ella, life flows like the music you love. Just as you transition between chords and melodies, you must also transition with life's changing rhythms."

A decade later, at 55, Ella's struggles continued and had taken a tremendous toll on her physically, mentally, and professionally. Unfortunately, her experience is all too familiar: the optimistic aspirations of youth meet the complex realities of life. That's because life combines the good and the bad—the ups and downs, the highs and lows. While talent, hope, and optimism are a good start, our resilience, adaptability, and mindset ultimately determine how far we go.

Like Ella, staying positive during the good times is easy, but what matters most is how we cope and respond when persistent challenges test our resolve.

Rethinking Our Approach to Change

Transformational leaders don't just deal with change; they leverage it. Instead of seeing change as a hurdle, they view it as an opportunity to innovate and progress. They don't merely adapt or find workarounds; they harness change to amplify their leadership and spark creativity.

Recognizing and welcoming change is not just beneficial; it's vital. An inability to navigate change can sink even the most promising careers. Take Ella, for example, whose personal and professional resistance to change was a life-defining setback. Despite her potential, she became paralyzed by the unfamiliar, limiting her overall impact.

To navigate change successfully, we must redefine our understanding of it. And this begins by understanding that our responses are choices. Charles Swindoll once said, "Life is 10% what happens to us and 90% how we respond." This wisdom continues to serve as a guiding principle in my life, business, and leadership. Remember, it's not the challenges that shape us but how we respond.

Delving Deep into the Root Cause

But beyond our perception of change, there's another influence: self-limiting beliefs. These assumptions about ourselves and the world prevent us from achieving our full potential. Without self-awareness or a reflective nature, these destructive beliefs can go unnoticed and persist indefinitely.

It's important to understand that, whether accurate reflections of reality or complete distortions, they profoundly influence our actions and impede our ability to adapt to change. Moreover, they often take hold during childhood, long before we realize they exist. Take, for instance, a child whose parents work multiple jobs to provide for them. Since they're seldom home, the child internalizes, "I must be unworthy of their time." Even when that child grows up and understands that their parents' absence was a necessary sacrifice, those early feelings of neglect persist. These beliefs are seldom rooted in our professional experiences. Still, they infiltrate every facet of our lives, casting shadows over our potential.

Ella's story, for instance, is about more than just struggling with change. Buried deep in her past were traumatic events that gave rise to the self-limiting beliefs that significantly impacted her professional journey. In her teens, she lost her younger brother in a car accident, followed by losing her aunt to breast cancer just five months later. As she cared for her elderly parents and raised her young son two decades later, she was subconsciously terrified of losing them to tragedy.

Recognizing this is crucial, but it's even more important to understand that what we focus on amplifies in significance. Dwelling on a problem only magnifies its emotional weight; conversely, confronting issues head-on empowers us. The same challenge can yield starkly different outcomes, depending on our approach.

From Recognition to Renewal

Learning the origins of our harmful limiting beliefs is pivotal. Yet, these insights are only the beginning; transformative change demands actionable steps that take these beliefs from recognition to renewal. As we've discussed, limiting beliefs are substantial barriers that hamper growth;

this may manifest as self-sabotaging thoughts, feelings of inadequacy, or adopting a limited worldview. I began the chapter with a cautionary tale, so I'd like to end with an uplifting story of what's possible when we defeat self-limiting beliefs.

Sarah grew up in a small town where, as a child, she was constantly reminded that girls grow up to be mothers and wives, not much else. Over time, she internalized this message, casting shadows over her dreams. However, as adolescence blossomed, so did Sarah's love for environmental science. But whenever she daydreamed of pursuing a degree or making a difference, those deep-seated beliefs crept in, echoing: "Girls don't do things like that."

Then, a chance encounter with a visiting lecturer at her school introduced her to environmental advocacy. Inspired, Sarah began the challenging task of unpacking her limiting beliefs. Here's her proactive, four-pronged approach:

1. **Challenge the Source:** Instead of blindly accepting her town's perspective, Sarah dissected its origins. She wondered if their beliefs were rooted in fact or merely echoed outdated norms. Her findings? These beliefs were baseless. Identifying and disproving this myth was pivotal in shattering it.

2. **Reflect and Reframe:** Sarah poured her fears, hopes, and dreams into her journal. Documenting her journey, she spotted the patterns of societal conditioning that had shaped her views, but also discovered moments of great strength, passion, and potential. Over time, her journal turned into a space of self-reflection and empowerment. She reshaped the narrative of her life, redefining what a girl "like her" could accomplish.

3. **Create New Beliefs:** Rejecting her old story, Sarah penned a new one. She began reshaping her narrative and developing new beliefs. No longer was she a girl confined by societal norms. Instead, she envisioned herself as an environmental changemaker.

4. **Seek Inspiration:** Immersing herself in the stories of female environmentalists, Sarah drew strength from their journeys. Whenever she came across an inspiring quote or a success story, it strengthened her resolve to pursue her dreams, irrespective of the limiting beliefs she once held.

Sarah received a scholarship to study environmental science at a prominent university. Today, Sarah is a leading voice in the field of sustainable agriculture. She didn't just break the mold; she shattered it. Her journey wasn't without its challenges, but by confronting her limiting beliefs, Sarah discovered a path she never thought possible. Her story isn't just compelling; it's transformative. It's a powerful reminder that the journey from recognition to renewal requires determination, introspection, and proactive change.

While this may sound simple, facing distressing issues and navigating emotional responses is far from effortless. Yet, the dividends far outweigh the discomfort and challenges.

It's easy to fall into the trap of thinking we lack limiting beliefs; after all, admitting vulnerability is difficult. While your limiting beliefs may not match Sarah's, you likely hold worldviews or perspectives that do not support your goal of becoming a transformational leader. Embracing hard truths is tough but essential.

And if not now, when?

15

The Heartbeat of Leadership: Cultivating Emotional Intelligence in a Digital Age

IQ and technical skills are important, but emotional intelligence is the Sine Qua Non of leadership.

—Daniel Goleman

SMARTPHONES. SEARCH ENGINES. Social media. Artificial intelligence. Not only have recent technological advances made it possible to access a world of information, remain connected like never before, and tap into a source of intelligence that far exceeds our own, but it's all in the palm of our hands.

To quote American novelist Anne Lamott, "It's a great time to be alive."[1] But is it? With technology and the free flow of information hailed as the great equalizer, younger generations should have a distinct advantage in producing some of history's most transformative leaders. But this assumption ignores an unescapable truth: leaders are not machines that run on data sets and communicate in binary code; they're human beings. As such, the endless flow of news, social pressure, and screen time have real-world consequences.

The National Institute of Mental Health reports that 33.7% of young adults and 49.5% of adolescents struggle with mental health issues, compared to just 28.1% of adults.[2] A 2018 study from the American Psychological Association revealed depression, anxiety, and self-harm are increasing in Generation Z and that 45% of young people "say social media makes them feel judged."[3] Combine these alarming statistics with the National Library of Medicine's findings that excessive screen time decreases the speed at which young adults can differentiate between happy and angry faces, and a disturbing trend emerges: reliance on technology is making human emotion increasingly difficult to perceive, interpret, and act on.[4]

It was inevitable that the warmth of human connections would gradually give way to the cold realities of digital interactions. This pattern of depersonalization is concerning; it's time for more leaders to cultivate emotional intelligence, a skill that, despite being undervalued, is central to transformative leadership.

Emotional Intelligence: The Cornerstone of Leadership

Coined in the early 1990s by psychologists Peter Salovey and John Mayer, *emotional intelligence* refers to our capacity to recognize and control emotional responses and handle interpersonal relationships with empathy, kindness, and understanding.[5] It's a concept that shares various abilities with effective leadership, including self-awareness, self-regulation, motivation, empathy, and social skills. Nearly a decade after Salovey and Mayer, psychologist Daniel Goleman published an article in the *Harvard Business Review* that forever linked emotional intelligence with leadership, writing, "The most effective leaders are alike in one crucial way: they all have a high degree of what has come to be known as emotional intelligence."[6]

Leaders with heightened emotional intelligence are attuned to the undercurrents of social situations, making them adept at conflict resolution. While intuitively understanding body language helps foster trust and makes it possible to connect with others, how do these skills translate in a digital landscape when significant misunderstandings are just a misinterpreted text away? Emotional intelligence remains an asset in discerning intent, tone, and emotion, even without face-to-face communication.

How valuable is emotional intelligence, and can it make a difference? Riverside Elementary was overcrowded with declining academic performance, frequent disciplinary issues, and a teacher turnover rate 5× the national average. The community had long lost faith in the institution, and students felt disconnected from their education and one another. After cycling through four principles in as many years, the district hired Jose Martinez, a seasoned administrator with a reputation for turning around struggling schools. However, his approach was different than most in the community had expected; instead of focusing on academics and discipline, Martinez prioritized emotional intelligence.

He held town hall meetings in his first week, inviting teachers, staff, students, and parents. He listened intently to their complaints, frustrations, and hopes. Students spoke of feeling unsupported, unheard, and unsafe; parents echoed these concerns and pleaded with school officials to create a more inclusive, understanding environment.

Using this feedback, Principal Martinez developed two new programs centered on emotional intelligence. Recognizing that teachers were the key to this significant cultural shift, he had a team of experts conduct training emphasizing empathy, active listening, and effective communication. First, he implemented a school-wide open forum that allowed students an hour each Friday morning to discuss their concerns, challenges, and successes with teachers and administrators. Next, he announced the implementation of the school's first peer mentorship program. The popular undertaking paired older students with younger ones for academic support and emotional guidance. These initiatives fostered a sense of community and belonging throughout the hallways and classrooms.

The transformation was remarkable. Within a year, disciplinary issues had decreased by nearly 60%, academic performance improved by an average of two letter grades, and teacher turnover rates plummeted. But the most telling sign of Riverside's renewal came during the annual community festival. While the school had long been a venue for the festivities, it was suddenly the heart of the celebration. Students showcased projects that blended academics with personal experiences, and the community rallied around their school with newfound pride.

Principal Martinez's success wasn't due to his expertise as an educator but a level of emotional intelligence that allowed him to connect with the school community, identify underlying issues, and implement lasting changes. The story of Riverside serves as a testament to the power of prioritizing empathy and fostering an environment in which individuals thrive, and communities come together.

The Gap Between Knowledge and Application

We must recognize and manage our emotions to reach our full potential as leaders. A comprehensive study of over a million people revealed that 90% of top performers exhibit high emotional intelligence, underscoring the link between emotional intelligence and effective leadership.[7] Why is this connection so strong? Because, as we've discussed, leadership no longer adheres to a hierarchical model that only emphasizes power and technical proficiency; the traditional approach of command and control has transitioned toward leadership that emphasizes collaboration and emotional intuition. Adopting this transition cultivates a work environment characterized by inclusivity, innovative ideas, creative thinking, and increased productivity.

Interacting with executives worldwide, I've noticed a recurring theme: leaders who undervalue emotional intelligence overestimate the amount they possess. Is this confined to a particular demographic or experience level? No, it's pervasive across all industries and responsibility levels. Still, leaders everywhere are becoming more aware of emotional intelligence, but there remains a gap between recognition and application. Why is there such a disconnect? Here are some insights:

- **Education's Missed Opportunity:** Our education system misses the mark by not embedding emotional intelligence as a core competency. By the time we enter the professional world, we're playing catch-up on skills vital for success.
- **Misunderstood Components:** There's a prevalent misperception about the components of emotional intelligence and its influence on behavior. Without a clear understanding, the journey to enhance this type of intelligence becomes muddled.
- **The Comfort Zone Conundrum:** Delving into emotional intelligence requires introspection and self-awareness, which can be uncomfortable. Humans naturally gravitate toward comfort, making this journey challenging for many.

- **The Cognitive–Emotional Fallacy:** There's a lingering belief that a high intelligence quotient, more commonly called IQ, compensates for a lack of emotional intelligence. While this may have been debatable in the past, today's interconnected world demands a balance.
- **The Quick-Fix Mentality:** There's a festering expectation of instant gratification in today's culture, but developing emotional intelligence is a continuous journey, not a one-time training session. Many leaders and organizations invest in short-term workshops, expecting an immediate transformation, only to be disappointed when deep-rooted behaviors don't change overnight.
- **Overemphasis on Hard Metrics:** Many organizations heavily base performance evaluations on metrics such as sales figures, project completions, and other tangible outcomes. While these are undoubtedly important, they often overshadow the equally crucial aspects of collaboration, conflict resolution, and interpersonal effectiveness. This imbalance leads to the unintentional neglect of emotional intelligence.
- **Misconception of Inherence:** There's a prevailing belief that emotional intelligence, like personality traits, is static and inherent. "You either have it or you don't." This misconception deters many from trying as it promotes the idea that some people are just not wired that way. While some naturally exhibit more, emotional intelligence is a skill that we can cultivate and refine with conscious effort and practice.

So, what's the real-world impact of emotional intelligence? Research suggests that cognitive intelligence accounts for only 20% of our long-term success. The lion's share, the remaining 80%, is influenced by emotional intelligence. Data from TalentSmartEQ indicates that the latter affects nearly 60% of performance across all professional roles. Emotional intelligence plays a pivotal role in job performance and leadership efficacy, and affects earnings; those with higher emotional intelligence average an additional $29,000 annually. With each point increase, the annual salary boost is around $1,300. The power of emotional intelligence in leadership is undeniable. It's not just about understanding emotions; it's about leveraging them for better decision-making, effective leadership, and overall success.[8]

The Five Pillars of Emotional Intelligence

Now, let's examine how the five pillars of emotional intelligence impact leadership and why those who cultivate them are more likely to inspire, connect, and empower others. This section is your chance to learn more about these and implement that knowledge.

1. Self-Awareness

Self-awareness is a fundamental component of emotional intelligence, serving as the bedrock for effective leadership. In this context, self-aware leaders can identify and label their emotions while accurately predicting how these developing emotions affect themselves and others. The capacity for introspection enables them to navigate challenges with resilience, utilize their strengths, address their shortcomings, and ingrain a culture of ongoing self-improvement, accountability, and transparency throughout the organization or team. Self-aware leaders offer steady direction and stability instead of letting shifting emotional currents carry them away.

Action Step: 360-Degree Feedback Exercise: One of the most effective ways to bolster self-awareness is to request feedback from a diverse group of colleagues, superiors, friends, and family. This comprehensive feedback mechanism gives leaders a mirror that helps them understand external perceptions in various professional and personal contexts.

For instance, consider the case of Melissa, a department head at a tech firm. While she considered herself a hands-on leader, feedback from her team revealed they often felt micromanaged. By engaging in the 360-degree feedback process, Melissa identified a gap between her self-perception and her team's experience. Armed with this insight, she adjusted her management style, fostering a more empowering environment for her team. Team productivity and morale improved over time, and Melissa had more time to strategize and innovate rather than get lost in the details.

2. Self-Regulation

Self-regulation refers to the ability to control and regulate one's emotions. This entails effectively managing emotional stress, displaying composure during stressful circumstances, and exercising self-control over impulses, enabling leaders to balance immediate demands and long-term objectives. Self-regulating leaders keep their emotions in check and think before acting. Such leaders foster an environment where people feel comfortable expressing ideas and taking calculated risks. They also inspire team confidence. Self-regulation is a critical psychological mechanism that empowers leaders to navigate uncertain and volatile situations effectively by maintaining emotional stability and mental clarity.

Action Step: Emotional Pause Technique: Practicing the emotional pause technique is a practical method to enhance self-regulation. This involves pausing, breathing, and reflecting before reacting to a stimulus, especially in high-stress situations. By mastering their impulses and reactions, leaders can create an environment of trust, learning, and adaptability, promoting individual and collective growth.

Luke is a project manager for a fast-paced logistics company. During a critical project phase, a team member made an error that significantly delayed delivery. Luke's initial impulse was to react with frustration. However, practicing the emotional pause technique, he took a deep breath and counted to 10 before assessing the situation. Instead of assigning blame, he gathered his team, addressed the issue collaboratively, and found a solution. This approach resolved the immediate problem and ensured that the team member responsible for the error learned from the mistake without feeling embarrassed or alienated.

3. Motivation

Motivation is the driving force that pushes people to work toward their goals. Extrinsic factors like material wealth or social status are less motivating for people with higher levels of emotional intelligence than intrinsic factors like self-improvement, fulfillment, and purpose. Their unyielding enthusiasm and commitment are the emotional triggers facilitating collaboration and promoting shared vision—the building blocks of achieving greatness. These leaders seek to achieve their aspirations, and align themselves with the goals and objectives of their team and organization.

Action Step: Personal Vision Board Exercise: Creating a personal vision board is a powerful way to tap into intrinsic motivation. This visual representation of your aspirations, dreams, and goals is a daily reminder of what truly matters beyond the immediate and tangible. By aligning personal passions with broader goals, individuals can create a lasting impact for themselves and their communities.

Maya is a young woman who's passionate about environmental conservation. While she had a stable job and a comfortable life, she felt a calling to make a difference in the world. To channel her motivation, Maya created a vision board with images of pristine forests, wildlife, community gatherings, and quotes about sustainability. Every morning, she'd spend a few minutes looking at her board, reigniting her passion and reminding herself of her larger purpose.

One day, inspired by her vision board, Maya organized a community clean-up drive in her local park. The small initiative soon became a community-wide movement, with neighbors regularly gathering to maintain shared spaces. Maya's intrinsic motivation, amplified by her vision board, led her to personal fulfillment and created a ripple effect, inspiring an entire community to come together for a shared cause.

4. Empathy

Leaders' ability to empathize with their team members is a hallmark of their emotional intelligence. Leaders who sympathize with their team members' experiences, challenges, and emotions foster trust, loyalty, and dedication. Emotionally intelligent leaders can tailor their approach to provide essential support, guidance, and inspiration by working to understand their team members' needs and concerns. When leaders reveal authentic compassion, their selflessness has a ripple effect within an organization, catalyzing inclusivity and mutual respect.

Action Step: Active Listening Sessions: One of the most effective ways to cultivate empathy is by practicing active listening. This involves fully concentrating, understanding, and responding to what someone says rather than passively "hearing" their message. By taking the time to understand and support those they lead, leaders can create environments where individuals feel valued, understood, and empowered to reach their full potential.

Jameson is a youth soccer coach. One of his players, Liam, had been underperforming during games and seemed disengaged during practices. Jameson pulled Liam aside after training instead of reprimanding him or making assumptions. During their conversation, the coach practiced active listening, giving Liam undivided attention without interrupting. Liam explained how his challenges at school affected his confidence on the field. Truly listening enabled Jameson to understand the root of Liam's struggles, offer support, and connect him with much-needed resources. It also allowed him to adjust his coaching style and help rebuild the player's confidence.

Liam's performance improved the following season, and the team culture seemed more cohesive and supportive. Jameson's empathetic approach, initiated by active listening, set a tone of understanding and compassion for the entire team.

5. Social Skills

Social skills are the ability of a leader to build and maintain relationships within their sphere of influence. This requires clear communication and the ability to resolve conflicts, influence others, and promote collaboration. Leaders with strong social skills can transform diverse personalities into cohesive, high-performing teams that leverage collective strength to achieve shared goals. It enables leaders to use the nuances of social interaction to navigate complex interpersonal dynamics with grace and empathy. As part of a leadership style that embraces the tenets of emotional intelligence, it fosters a positive, inclusive environment in which everyone feels heard, understood, and valued.

Action Step: Regular Team Building: One of the most effective ways to hone social skills is by engaging in team-building exercises that foster communication, confidence, and engagement. Furthermore, these activities allow leaders to understand and connect with team members. By fostering an environment that emphasizes communication, trust, and collaboration, leaders can bring out the best in their teams, ensuring both individual growth and collective success.

Consider the story of Jesse, a scoutmaster who led a pack of enthusiastic young adventurers; the problem was that the group struggled to work together. Jesse introduced regular team-building exercises during weekend camping trips, recognizing the need to strengthen their social cohesion. One such activity had teams of two racing to set up their tents, with one member blindfolded and the other giving verbal directions. This required clear communication, trust, and collaboration—not to mention it was funny to watch.

By summer's end, the team dynamic had transformed. The scouts learned to communicate more effectively, trust each other's expertise, and work together to overcome challenges. Jesse's emphasis on building social skills improved the group's efficiency and created an environment where each scout felt a sense of belonging and camaraderie.

Embracing Emotional Intelligence in a Digital World

In the heart of Silicon Valley, where algorithms and cutting-edge technologies reign supreme, Satya Nadella's story stands out. Nadella, the CEO of Microsoft, shared a transformative moment from early in his career when he was hyper-focused on hard metrics. This was how he gauged success until a leadership seminar made him realize the importance of introducing empathy and understanding into the workplace. This shift in perspective became instrumental in reshaping Microsoft's culture. Under Nadella's leadership, Microsoft transitioned from a company known for its internal competitiveness to one that prioritizes collaboration, learning, and growth. Instead of a new technology or groundbreaking product driving this transformation, it resulted from Nadella's emphasis on emotional intelligence.[9]

Nadella's story underscores a vital point: even in industries dominated by technology, the human element—our ability to connect, understand, and empathize—remains our most valuable asset. As the World Economic Forum highlighted in 2020, emotional intelligence isn't just nice to have; it's one of the top 10 crucial skills needed for success in the modern workplace.[10] While some might naturally be more attuned to it, the beauty of emotional intelligence is that anyone can develop and refine it.

In an era where digital interactions have become the norm, leaders must intentionally cultivate their emotional intelligence. This means dedicating time to introspection, actively seeking feedback, and continuously learning from diverse perspectives. It's not just about staying relevant; it's about leading with authenticity, understanding, and vision. As we navigate this digital age, let's remember the examples of empathetic leadership set by transformative leaders like Principal Martinez from Riverside Elementary and Satya Nadella from Microsoft.

It is a powerful reminder that while algorithms and data might shape the world, emotional intelligence will lead us into the future.

16

Authentic Leadership: Leading with Integrity

Look for three things in people: Intelligence, energy, and integrity. And if they don't have the last one, don't even bother with the first two.

—Warren Buffet

FEW THINGS ARE as powerful as remaining true to oneself and facing each day with integrity. But even for those who pride themselves on being authentic, the siren call of professional power, influence, and prestige can overshadow their core values. As such, we do not define leaders by their rise to prominence, but rather by their ability to resist external pressures at the top, where temptation is strongest.

Throughout history, accomplished leaders have reached positions of great power and influence, only to fall from grace after compromising their principles. This includes political leaders like President Richard Nixon and South Korea's Park Geun-hye, sports superstars such as Lance Armstrong, Pete Rose, and Barry Bonds, and business leaders like Wells Fargo CEO John Stumpf and Turing Pharmaceutical's founder Martin Shkreli. The tragedy is that when those in positions of power stray from their core beliefs, it's not just their reputations that suffer; they also jeopardize entire organizations and put the livelihoods of thousands at risk.

Case in point: the 2008 financial crisis was a devastating event that shattered countless dreams and caused widespread pain and despair. Beyond the headlines of chaos and economic turmoil lies the truth: the crisis wasn't the result of innocent financial missteps, but a lapse in integrity.

Enter Lehman Brothers, a name synonymous with the financial meltdown. The firm's inability to react to impending risk was due to a dangerous blend of overconfidence and greed that started with the firm's CEO, Richard Fuld, and quickly infected the entire company. He overlooked crucial warning signs and let significant financial issues fester and grow.

Even when trouble became apparent, Fuld declined external help and capital, maintaining that Lehman was a dominant industry force that could handle any challenge. However, as the crisis escalated, Lehman's vulnerabilities became undeniable, and the firm had no choice but to file for bankruptcy. Lehman Brothers' collapse and the global devastation it caused is a cautionary tale of leaders prioritizing personal gain over the greater good. It's a powerful reminder that integrity and honesty aren't optional virtues, but the bedrock of society. At the heart of such monumental failures is the intoxicating allure of power. Ascending to such positions requires immense effort, resilience, and sacrifice, but the pressures at the top can cloud one's moral compass. We must recognize that few leaders embark on their journeys intending to be dishonest or knowingly cause harm.[1]

This inadvertent drift is why we must conduct regular self-assessments and practice honest self-reflection. Recognizing our values and crafting a leadership brand rooted in authenticity isn't easy; it demands time, introspection, and commitment. Finding answers and establishing ethical boundaries is an intense process of self-discovery that, for some, takes longer; in no way does this reflect negatively on a person's sincerity. All that matters is that we put in the work and never compromise our principles. While cliché, authentic leadership is a journey, not a destination.

The Foundational Core

The beauty of leadership, much like success, is that there are countless paths to achievement and even more to making a lasting impact.

I'm willing to bet many people have influenced you, each leaving a small piece of themselves in you. That's because our relationships, regardless of perceived importance, impact who we become. This is why you'll often hear leaders recommend surrounding yourself with those you want to emulate—success breeds success.

Reflecting on my athletic journey, several coaches have made such an impact that I still recognize parts of them in me. One was loud and enthusiastic, igniting my passion and motivating me like no one else could. Another was calm yet connected, pulling the best out of me when others had failed to do so. Then there are those special people whose influence changes your life; topping that list is my grandmother, whose quiet, unwavering strength helped define me as a person and a leader.

These individuals were all very different from one another, yet each succeeded. The same is true of leadership; while tried-and-true methods exist, there's no universal approach to success. What works for one leader may not work for another. However, core principles regarding integrity never change. Here are my top six:

1. It's never the wrong time to do the right thing.
2. Your private actions are as important as what you do in public.
3. Staying true to your values is a gift. Never let it go.
4. It's not enough to win; you also must win honorably.
5. A well-lived life is more admirable than one filled with success and regret.
6. Your reputation is fragile; it takes years to build but moments to shatter.

Keep these principles in mind as you navigate your leadership journey. While many more are out there, these six provide a solid foundation. As aspirations grow, so does the likelihood of temptation and flawed judgment. Nobody is powerful enough to evade accountability forever, a lesson highlighted by the controversy surrounding Hall of Fame college basketball coach Rick Pitino.

In 2017, when Pitino was head coach of the University of Louisville basketball team, he became the focus of a federal fraud and corruption investigation. The investigation revealed that several coaches, including members of Pitino's staff, had worked with Adidas executives to funnel money to the families of high-profile recruits in exchange for their commitment to play at Adidas-sponsored schools.

Although Pitino denied knowledge of the scheme, evidence suggested that he was not only aware of it, but possibly involved. In one instance, the Federal Bureau of Investigation (FBI) had wiretaps of an Adidas executive discussing funneling $100,000 to the family of a top recruit to ensure he would attend Louisville; Pitino was identified as "Coach 2" on the recording, which proved his involvement.

As a result of the scandal, the university fired Pitino for cause in October 2017. The University of Louisville also faced severe National Collegiate Athletics Association (NCAA) penalties, including the vacation of their 2013 NCAA Men's Basketball Championship. What made his fall from grace even worse was his respected stature in the basketball world. The scandal tarnished his legacy and highlighted severe ethical issues in college athletics.[2]

Code of Leadership

Earlier in the chapter, I mentioned that most leaders don't start intending to engage in unethical behavior, harm others, and destroy their careers—so why does it happen? Because as time passes, leaders grow increasingly susceptible to the trappings of power, authority, and notoriety. When someone spends decades having everyone around them affirm their greatness, they not only begin to believe it, but also lose touch with reality and become addicted to the attention.

Celebrities serve as a great example; it's hard to think of an A-list actor who, after a long career, comes out the other side unaffected. When people begin believing that they're special, they gradually lose their moral bearings and give in to the seduction of immediate gratification.

It's simply not enough to know right from wrong or to talk about the value of integrity; we must become intentional about maturing into authentic leaders who hold sacred the honor we are entrusted to protect. But how? By adopting a leadership code and keeping it at the forefront of everything you do. Here are the five pillars of every great leader.

1. The Heartbeat of Leadership: Self-Awareness

The importance of self-awareness cannot be overstated, as it's the heartbeat that sustains a leader's integrity. It is the process through which leaders gain insight into their values, beliefs, attitudes, biases, and behaviors. This lays the foundation on which we build authenticity.

The Significance of Self-Awareness:

- **Aligning with Values:** Knowing what you believe, stand for, and value facilitates the alignment of decision-making with these principles, fostering an environment of integrity.
- **Understanding Biases:** Leaders are not exempt from biases. Self-awareness helps us recognize and address biases affecting our judgment and interactions with others.
- **Enhancing Emotional Intelligence:** A heightened sense of self-awareness contributes to improved emotional intelligence, which is crucial for managing one's emotions and understanding the feelings of others.
- **Welcoming Feedback:** Self-awareness enhances a leader's receptivity to feedback. This is vital since understanding different perspectives allows leaders to adjust their actions accordingly. Encourage input from colleagues, subordinates, and superiors.

Cultivating Self-Awareness:

- **Reflection and Journaling:** Dedicate time for regular self-reflection. Reflect on your actions, decisions, and interactions with others. Analyzing situations can provide valuable insights into your behavior and reactions. Keeping a journal to document your experiences, emotions, and reflections can be a helpful tool for tracking personal growth and recognizing behavior patterns.
- **Mindfulness and Meditation:** Mindfulness practices, such as meditation, deep breathing, and yoga, can enhance self-awareness by promoting a deeper connection between mind and body.
- **Professional Coaching:** Consider engaging with a professional coach who can provide objective feedback and strategies for personal development.

- **Educational Workshops and Books:** Enroll in workshops or read books about self-awareness, emotional intelligence, and leadership development. Continuous learning is vital to enhancing self-awareness.

The journey toward increased self-awareness is continuous and marked by curiosity, openness, and the willingness to evolve. As leaders nurture their self-awareness, they bolster their integrity and cultivate an environment of honesty, respect, and shared growth. Through this proactive endeavor, leaders are better positioned to navigate the complexities of ethical leadership.

2. The Mirror of Leadership: Transparency

Leaders who are transparent about their decisions and expectations foster a culture of trust and openness. But what do I mean by transparency being the mirror of leadership? Simple: a focus on transparency reflects a leader's ethos and values while providing clarity and understanding to those they lead. It's an open book where decisions, processes, and challenges are shared, promoting engagement and shared responsibility.

The Significance of Transparency:

- **Trust-Building:** Transparency is the cornerstone of trust. When leaders are open about their actions and decisions, it instills a sense of confidence among team members.
- **Improved Communication:** Transparent leadership fosters an environment of open communication, encouraging team members to express their ideas and concerns freely.
- **Increased Engagement:** When leadership is transparent, team members are more engaged since they feel like part of the team.
- **Ethical Decision-Making:** Transparency promotes an ethical culture by reducing the chances of hidden agendas and encouraging honest discussion on various organizational issues.

Cultivating Transparency:

- **Honesty in Reporting:** Be honest about how things are going, whether positive or negative. Honest reporting establishes credibility and earns respect.
- **Involve Others in Decision-Making:** Involve team members in your decision-making processes, especially when the decisions impact them. This inclusion not only promotes transparency but also collective ownership.
- **Admit Mistakes:** No one is infallible. When mistakes occur, admit them openly and use them as teaching moments for the team.
- **Regular Updates:** Hold meetings to update the team about organizational changes, challenges, and successes.

The road toward transparency has its bumps, but the result is honest, engaged, high-performing teams. Through fostering transparency, leaders uphold the principle of integrity and create a legacy of trust and openness that resonates with everyone involved.

3. The Pillar of Leadership: Accountability

Accepting responsibility for actions and decisions, especially during challenging times, is a hallmark of a leader's integrity. By doing so, you model the importance of accountability, demonstrate that mistakes are natural, and cultivate a team culture of trust, respect, and reliability.

The Significance of Accountability:

- **Trust and Reliability:** When leaders demonstrate accountability, it fosters a sense of trust and reliability among their teams. It signals that they can be counted on to honor their commitments.
- **Enhanced Performance:** Accountability helps set clear expectations, leading to enhanced performance as individuals are aware of the consequences of their actions and decisions.
- **Learning and Improvement:** Owning up to mistakes creates a culture where learning and continuous improvement are encouraged.

- **Increased Engagement:** When leaders exhibit accountability, it encourages a similar level of responsibility among their team, leading to increased engagement and a cohesive environment.

Cultivating Accountability:

- **Set Clear Expectations:** Clearly articulate what is expected from each team member, ensuring they understand their responsibilities and the standards they must meet.
- **Celebrate Successes:** Acknowledge and celebrate when team members meet or exceed expectations, reinforcing a culture of accountability.
- **Set the Example:** Be the model of accountability for your team; your actions set the tone.
- **Utilize Technology:** Employ tools and platforms that track performance and make contributions and progress visible.

Embedding accountability into leadership bolsters individual and organizational integrity and propels collective growth and success. Through actionable steps and a conscious effort toward embracing responsibility, leaders can significantly impact their ability to remain ethical. Through this endeavor, they step closer to creating a legacy of trust, respect, and exemplary leadership.

4. The Essence of Leadership: Humility

Humility is a profound strength in leadership. It takes humility to acknowledge one's limitations, admit mistakes, and prioritize the needs of others over self-interest. Humble leaders are self-aware, open to feedback, and committed to the betterment of those they lead. Their humility humanizes them, making them approachable and helping to foster collaboration.

The Significance of Humility:

- **Fostering a Learning Environment:** Humble leaders are open to new ideas and perspectives, creating a conducive atmosphere for learning and growth.

- **Promoting Collaboration:** By valuing the contributions of others, humble leaders enhance teamwork and collaboration within the organization.
- **Increasing Resilience:** Accepting failures and setbacks with a constructive mindset nurtures further resilience and growth.
- **Driving Authentic Leadership:** Humility is integral to authentic leadership, encouraging leaders to be genuine and transparent in their interactions.

Cultivating Humility:

- **Acknowledge the Contributions of Others:** Regularly recognize and appreciate the efforts and accomplishments of your team.
- **Admit Mistakes:** When you make a mistake, admit it openly and use it as a stepping stone toward improvement.
- **Practice Gratitude:** Cultivate a habit of expressing gratitude and reflecting humility.
- **Avoid Hubris:** Monitor your behavior to guard against arrogance or the assumption that you have all the answers.

Embarking on a journey toward humble leadership is making a personal and professional commitment to move beyond ego-driven practices. The infusion of humility significantly enhances the team's vibrancy, creativity, and inclusivity, crafting a legacy of impact and respect.

5. The True Nature of Leadership: Service

Putting people first is about shifting the focus from self-interest to the well-being and success of others. Service-oriented leaders prioritize the needs of their team and the broader community, creating a supportive environment that empowers others to thrive. This approach aligns with ethical standards, promotes trust, and improves outcomes. Leaders who serve see beyond the transactional value of their roles and invest in understanding their team members' unique contributions, aspirations, and well-being. By doing so, they not only enrich the lives of others but also broaden the path of influence and impact they have as leaders.

The Significance of Service:

- **Inspiring Loyalty:** When leaders prioritize service over self-interest, it fosters loyalty and trust among team members, paving the way for collaboration.
- **Fostering Empowerment:** Leaders empower others to reach their full potential and contribute meaningfully by serving others.
- **Promoting Ethical Behavior:** Service dovetails with ethical behavior, reinforcing fairness, respect, and integrity.
- **Boosting Productivity and Engagement:** When leaders are attuned to the needs and well-being of their team, it significantly enhances engagement and productivity.

Cultivating a Service-Based Mindset:

- **Empower Others:** Delegate responsibility, provide the necessary resources, and support individuals in pursuing their goals.
- **Practice Empathy and Compassion:** Display empathy and compassion in interactions, showing understanding and support during challenges.
- **Be Accessible:** Maintain an open-door policy, making yourself accessible to team members and promoting open communication.
- **Encourage a Service Mindset:** Promote service and cooperation within your team and the broader organization.

Service through leadership is about transcending personal ambitions to foster a culture of mutual respect, support, and shared success. Leaders embracing a service-oriented approach elevate their leadership practice and significantly contribute to creating a positive, collaborative, high-performing environment. As leaders prioritize others' interests over their own, they earn respect and synergize individual strengths toward collective goals.

PART

V

Sparking Transformation in Others

17

Unlocking the Power
of Inspirational Leadership

If your actions inspire others to dream more, learn more, and do more, you are a leader.

—John Quincy Adams

AN INSPIRATIONAL STORY has captured the nation's imagination as I write this. In some ways, it's the classic underdog story—like *The Bad News Bears* or *The Mighty Ducks*—had either film franchises involved college football and cast the legendary Deion Sanders as head coach. Besides that, the transformative journey of the University of Colorado football team reads like a Hollywood script, complete with a captivating superstar who's unapologetically unique, audaciously ambitious, and never lacks confidence.

In December 2022, Deion Sanders became the head coach of the Colorado Buffaloes, a team that had just come off an embarrassing 1–11 season. When the Hall of Famer came to Colorado, it wasn't to help a struggling team but to redefine it. Sanders set the tone during his first team address by announcing that things would change and encouraging those who couldn't meet his standards to transfer schools, advice most of the players took.

His approach, a radical break with tradition, was ridiculed by the sports media and drew outrage from head coaches across college football.

However, according to Fox Sports college football analyst Joel Klatt, critics were wrong. The media's narrative painted a picture of Sanders driving players out so that he could replace them, but this wasn't entirely accurate. According to Klatt, the coaching staff cut a few players, but the remainder chose to leave because of increased expectations and higher standards.[1]

Why does this example emphasize the significance of inspirational leadership? Is it that Deion Sanders, now known as Coach Prime, succeeds at everything he does? No. I chose it because, when you look beneath the surface, it's evident how much his players respect and admire him and how motivated they are by his compelling vision.

Coach Prime understands there's power in belonging and instills this mindset in those he leads. After all, bonds centered on the greater good or a higher cause are powerful and nearly impossible to break. To further imbue this sense of belonging in his players, Sanders leads them in proclaiming "We Believe" and "We Coming" after each victory. Reaffirming their loyalty to the team and each other when their systems are flooded with endorphins from winning is a potent combination. Few realize the scope of what's happening in Boulder, and what's happening is nothing short of remarkable.

Although there will always be critics, Coach Prime has shown himself to be an inspirational leader. Despite college football's rivalries, traditions, and allegiances, Sanders exhibits steadfast composure, directing his attention toward the bigger picture of his team's potential. His decision to overhaul the roster was risky, but it appears to be paying off. Despite the previous season's record, the players have renewed hope and ambition thanks to their coach's confidence. Deion Sanders is an example of having a conviction so compelling that others can't help but believe.

A Prerequisite for Leadership Excellence

Historically, leaders have regarded inspiring others as a secondary advantage, appreciated but not deemed necessary. Furthermore, society generally accepted that inspiring others consisted of delivering impassioned speeches or exhibiting a magnetic personality, qualities that people either possessed or didn't.

This fixed viewpoint is entirely at odds with reality in the modern, constantly evolving world. Not only is this statement false, but the ability to inspire others is vital to effective leadership, and the greater one's ability to inspire, the greater one's influence and impact. As we've mentioned, one leader's preferred method may be counterproductive for another. Becoming an inspirational leader has little to do with your personality—or the ability to deliver rousing speeches—and everything to do with knowing where inspiration comes from and how to apply it in your daily work.

How significant is being inspirational to a leader's success? Since this trait often characterizes the best and most influential leaders, it's safe to assume it's high on the list. The ability to inspire is necessary for becoming a great leader, whether in sports, business, community activism, politics, or education. Given the importance of inspirational leadership, what distinguishes truly inspiring leaders?

In 2013, Bain & Company set out to identify the foundation of inspirational leadership through an analytical strategy aimed at defining, measuring, and enhancing skills. The analysis identified 33 statistically significant attributes ranging from self-regard, which involves realistic confidence in one's abilities, to empowerment, which encourages a sense of autonomy and challenge. While possessing even one of these attributes doubles your chance of being inspiring, those with four or more are almost always considered highly inspirational. The key takeaway is that focusing on honing a few intrinsic strengths and mitigating weaknesses to a neutral level can significantly enhance your ability to inspire.[2]

Cultivating a Deeper Understanding

Having explored the significance of inspirational leadership, let's discuss what it takes to inspire. Leadership that brings out the best in others moves far beyond the superficial, reaching the core of what matters most. Let's look at a few popular misconceptions:

- **You must be an extrovert to inspire:** The spectrum of introversion and extroversion has little to do with our ability to inspire; it transcends these personality traits, focusing instead on the depth of connection we create with others.

- **All leaders are great orators:** While stirring speeches can move audiences, they're not a prerequisite for being inspirational. Inspiring others lies in the substance of your message.
- **You can fake it until you make it:** Inspiration cannot be faked or contrived; it's cultivated through genuine interactions and relationships.
- **Find a great leader and copy them:** Copying others in the hopes of becoming inspirational will surely fail. True inspiration stems from originality and conviction.
- **You must have a great voice and be refined to lead:** It's not your voice or presentation that others react to, but the authenticity and intent behind your words and actions.
- **Leaders must hold a title or position:** Your ability to inspire has nothing to do with your position; it's a trait that flourishes independent of hierarchical standings.

Inspiring others is more than winning or succeeding in your career. The ability to inspire is a priceless trait that helps you thrive regardless of the situation. At various life stages, the aspiration to be an inspiration to our children, family, friends, and the broader community is profound. It's not just about leading; it's about resonating on a deeper level that ignites change and spurs growth.

Common misinterpretations surrounding what it takes to inspire often blur the lines between motivation and inspiration. A spark of motivation can arise from almost anywhere—an energizing video, a collection of impactful quotes, or engaging in self-dialogue to embody desired traits. It's often an external push that ebbs and flows. We may feel motivated on a Monday, but it's gone two days later.

On the other hand, inspiration is not a mere stimulant; it's a core drive. It's that inner tug that keeps pulling you forward, fueling not just your actions but the pursuit of excellence that transforms ordinary jobs into meaningful vocations, projects into passions, and the adequate into the exceptional.

This narrative isn't about downplaying motivation; it's an essential aspect of the journey toward achievement. But it's imperative to comprehend the subtle yet profound distinctions between motivation and inspiration. While a spark serves as a starting point, the enduring allure of inspiration carves out truly impactful leaders and individuals who leave a lasting mark.

The Building Blocks of Inspirational Leadership

In an era marked by swift transformations and endless competition, the hallmark of enduring success transcends the conventional metrics of achievements. Transformative leadership is characterized not merely by expertise but also by its ability to inspire. No longer an ideal, being inspirational is a prerequisite for navigating modern-day challenges. Such leadership galvanizes teams and orchestrates innovation and resilience toward a broader horizon.

As with anything of value, developing the ability to inspire requires hard work and commitment. Here are eight core principles every leader must practice and actionable steps to help expand their ability to inspire:

1. Lead from the Front

Leading from the front showcases a level of commitment your team can't help but respect and creates a path they want to follow. Mary Barra's handling of the 2014 General Motors crisis exemplifies this principle. When the company received backlash for producing vehicles with faulty ignition switches, her decisive actions, public addresses, and willingness to take tough questions demonstrated a commitment to accountability and transparency. Barra's ability to lead from the front navigated the company through the crisis and restored public trust. It showcases the importance of leaders being at the forefront during challenging times with a blend of resilience, responsibility, and clear-headedness that resonates throughout the organization.[3]

Putting it into practice: Allocate time to work alongside your team because nothing inspires people like a leader willing to roll up their sleeves and get their hands dirty.

2. You Can Only Lead If Others Follow

Leadership is a two-way street; a leader's vision and actions should inspire trust and a willingness to follow. I discussed Satya Nadella a few chapters back, but here's another example of how his leadership has forever changed Microsoft. When Nadella became CEO, his growth mindset and emphasis on fostering a collaborative culture rejuvenated the organization.[4] His approachable and inclusive leadership style made it easier for employees to align with his vision. Most importantly, Nadella's vision was widely shared, which aided in driving a deeper connection. Others are likelier to commit and follow if they understand what is at stake and why. A leader's ability to demonstrate their commitment to building a supportive and inspiring environment paves the way for collective success.

Putting it into practice: Promote candid and clear communication by implementing an "open door" policy that encourages team members to express their ideas, concerns, or feedback. Proactively seek out others instead of passively waiting for them to approach you. Ask more questions. Arrange frequent meetings with individual team members to strengthen bonds, provide task clarity, and communicate how they contribute to the overarching vision.

3. Define Your Values and Live Them

Inspirational leaders have a clear set of values and principles that guide their decisions and actions. While many leaders enjoy engaging in culture-related discussions, the gap between what they say and what they do is often quite wide. It's not enough to have a set of shared values or principles; leaders must consistently live them and emphasize their importance. Netflix, for example, states that employees must be "extraordinarily candid with one another" because "we will learn faster and be better if we can make giving and receiving feedback less stressful and a more normal part of work life." They also believe their value of "avoid[ing] rules" is essential for sustaining adaptability considering shifting market conditions.[5] Leaders have a greater capacity to inspire others when they define values clearly and serve as role models for those around them.

Putting it into practice: Write down what you stand for and then regularly reflect on your actions to ensure they align with those values. Share your reflections with a mentor or trusted colleague and ask for honest insight. Define your values, live by them, and elaborate on their significance.

4. Create an Inspiring and Clear North Star

A clear vision is a North Star guiding you toward a common goal. Elon Musk's vision of a sustainable future and Mars's colonization reflect an inspiring level of clarity that mobilizes resources and efforts around achieving these goals. It exemplifies how a well-articulated vision can foster innovation, collaboration, and sustained growth, propelling organizations and teams into a new frontier of success.[6] Elon Musk can be a divisive figure; while public sentiment about him is subjective, there's no debating that his inspiring vision has allowed him to reach great heights. While a world-changing vision like Musk's isn't required, inspirational leadership requires a vision that inspires, engages, and unites.

Putting it into practice: Reiterate your North Star each morning, then check in with yourself at the end of the day to gauge if your actions align with that vision. Communicate how your North Star vision affects all parties involved and create a cadence for incorporating it into weekly and monthly meetings.

5. Catch People Doing the Right Thing

Nurturing dynamic relationships is more crucial than accomplishing tasks. During Indra Nooyi's 12-year tenure as CEO of PepsiCo, she wrote more than 400 letters annually to the parents of her direct reports, expressing gratitude for their respective sons' or daughters' hard work.[7] This heartwarming example of valuing relationships in a corporate setting enhanced workplace morale and created a culture of appreciation and respect that transcended professional boundaries. This principle underscores the significance of human connection in creating a productive work environment that inspires excellence.

Putting it into practice: Make it a habit to catch people doing the right thing. Acknowledge those who exemplify the effort, mindset, and actions to help the team, no matter how small the act. Building deeper relationships and expressing gratitude should be ongoing processes.

6. Focus on Results and People

James Zenger surveyed over 60,000 workers to find out what makes a great leader in the eyes of their subordinates. He found that result-oriented leaders had a 14% chance of being viewed as exceptional. Even worse, people-oriented leaders only had a 12% chance of being considered great. However, that figure skyrocketed to 72% when leaders adopted a dual focus on results and people.[8] Transformational leaders understand that while relentlessly driving results is critical, prioritizing and caring for the people responsible for executing them is equally important.

Putting it into practice: Foster an environment that encourages excellence while focusing equally on people. Ensure team members receive the necessary coaching to excel while remaining transparent about their goals using regular performance check-ins. Avoid engaging in personal attacks by focusing on fixing the issue instead of focusing on the individual.

7. Connect the Future to the Present

Strategic foresight is a hallmark of outstanding leadership. Jeff Bezos's long-term outlook with Amazon illustrates how planning for the future, even at the expense of short-term gains, can propel organizations to monumental success. From the outset, Bezos envisioned Amazon becoming "the world's most customer-centric company." This long-term vision guided the company's strategic decisions in the present, and prioritizing customer satisfaction over immediate financial gains helped the company build a loyal customer base.[9] Leaders with a future-oriented mindset are adept at identifying opportunities, anticipating challenges, and preparing for change, ensuring sustained growth and relevance. Inspiration is cultivated and cascaded when everyone knows what they are working toward and strategic goals are linked to present actions.

Putting it into practice: Consider strategic planning an ongoing process in which all parties involved help shape the future. Search for ways to connect your strategic objectives to the here and now through daily processes, metrics, and desired outcomes.

8. Set the Right Tone

Setting the right tone can significantly impact the atmosphere and outcomes in various group settings. A notable example is Erin Gruwell, a high school teacher whose story inspired the movie and book *Freedom*

Writers. Erin Gruwell started working as a teacher at the violent and gang-infested Woodrow Wilson High School in Long Beach, California, in the mid-1990s. Gruwell set a different tone from the outset; she exhibited respect, empathy, and high expectations for her students. She encouraged open dialogue, active learning, and reflection, promoting a safe, inclusive, and constructive classroom environment. Gruwell transformed a divided and disengaged group of students into a cohesive, motivated community of learners who transcended their challenges.[10] Leaders who set a positive tone encourage open communication, collaboration, and a shared sense of inspiration that can change everything.

Putting it into practice: Begin each day with a positive message or share success stories reinforcing the culture and values you aim to promote within your team or organization. It's always up to the leader to make the difference.

Inspirational Leadership Is a Responsibility

Each of these principles lays the cornerstone for forging a brand of leadership that is compelling, inspiring, and transformational. Leaders who practice these principles are on track to create a legacy of success, innovation, and positive change.

The significance of inspiration cannot be overstated; it triggers change, fuels innovation, and bridges the gap between ideas and action. Influential and transformational leaders take abstract ideas, clarify them, and instill hope and optimism in all. They make people believe in themselves, helping them overcome challenges and reach new heights. It's about creating a ripple effect of positivity and building a culture of continuous growth and collaborative success. Inspirational leaders don't just lead; they elevate everyone around them. They encourage people to think creatively, work together, and achieve great things. And this isn't just good for the short term; it builds a solid foundation for long-term success and a positive, thriving team culture.

As you walk the leadership path with these principles in mind, remember that your ability to inspire will have a lasting impact. The inspirational leader's responsibility is to serve those they lead and help them achieve more than they ever imagined possible.

18

Navigating Effective Communication

Before you can inspire with emotion, you must be swamped with it yourself. Before you can move their tears, your own must flow. To convince them, you must yourself believe.

—Winston Churchill

CAN YOU IMAGINE a world in which diamonds were as commonplace as quartz? Even those who know little about jewelry recognize the stone's value. While part of this is simple economics, namely, the principle of scarcity, it's also the result of deeply ingrained traditions and cultural popularity. The most prevalent is the diamond engagement ring, a tradition so powerful that even those who believe it to be ridiculous and archaic bend to the social pressures surrounding it.

But have you ever wondered how this tradition originated and why the stone in that ring isn't quartz? After all, diamond and quartz are minerals that retract and reflect light, hold chemically inactive properties, and rate highly on the Mohs Hardness Scale.

In the 1930s, the diamond industry experienced another potent economic principle: supply and demand. Technological advancements made it easier to mine and ship diamonds, thus flooding the market. This increase in availability happened at the same time the United States experienced a catastrophic economic downturn; prices fell. From 1929 to 1932, the U.K. Wholesale Price Index for rough diamonds plummeted by 42%, dropping from a rating of 100 to 58. Do you want to know how this precious stone went from an unwanted global commodity to symbolizing an institution as powerful as marriage? Advertising, of course.

Hard times fuel innovation and ingenuity. In this case, that fell to jewelry retailer De Beers, who forever changed how the world would think about diamonds with four little words: "A diamond is forever." Still in use today, this advertising slogan has proven to be the most successful in history. Why was it so effective, and what can we learn from it? Instead of trying to sell diamonds, De Beers sold something far more valuable: the promise of lasting love.[1]

You may be wondering about the connection between engagement rings and leadership communication. There isn't one, not directly. The lesson lies in effective communicators understanding their audience's desires, hopes, and fears well enough to weave captivating narratives that inspire, comfort, and seemingly speak to the individual.

After all, De Beers didn't achieve its objective by directly selling diamonds to customers. Instead, it used storytelling to make its product inseparable from one of life's happiest moments and connect it to the universal human need for companionship and acceptance—and that's what it sold. No matter what you think about marriage, diamonds, or even De Beers, there's no denying that what they accomplished is a masterclass in impactful communication and a brilliant demonstration of how narrative can inspire and shape social norms.

Effective communication is an absolute requirement for transformational leadership. The ability to articulate your vision, build trust, and inspire are hallmarks of an exceptional leader. This begins and ends with learning to be a skilled communicator. Let's say you have a brilliant mind with the potential to change the world and the skill set and vision to match. What good are they if you can't articulate and communicate them?

The Imperative of Effective Communication

The idea that leaders must communicate effectively is not some groundbreaking revelation. So, why does weak communication still permeate organizations worldwide if this is so well established? Understanding the importance of something doesn't necessarily equate to taking the action required to improve it. Simply knowing the value of effective communication isn't enough to create it; you can't just flip a switch to start communicating better once you're aware of the issue. Instead, this burden of knowledge greatly magnifies the inability of a team, organization, or individual to build culture, achieve objectives, and move with urgency.

Why does this matter? For starters, like everything else, it affects the bottom line. Researchers studied corporations with over 100,000 employees and found that poor communication costs large corporations an average of $60 million annually. While this isn't entirely shocking, the other half of their findings are. The study also revealed that ineffective communication costs small businesses nearly $500,000 annually. While it's a fraction of the money corporations lose, its relative impact is staggeringly more severe.[2]

The Economist Intelligence Unit of the Economist Group conducted a study exploring the disastrous impact of ineffective communication. The unit's research revealed that 52% of employees had added stress due to poor communication, 44% had a project fail or be delayed due to a collapse of communication, and 31% experienced lower morale due to inefficient communication.[3] Even more concerning, 69% of managers in a study reported by *Harvard Business Review* said they feel uncomfortable communicating with their employees.[4]

A leader's communication efficacy creates a pervasive ripple effect. Unfortunately, the behaviors causing poor communication are often deeply ingrained and difficult to change.

Unveiling the Perception Fallacy

During a company conference in Miami, I asked the audience, "How many of you believe there's a communication gap between those in this room and the team members who are not present?" Every leader in the room raised their hand. Why is this significant? Just a week prior, the company's CEO, COO, and two vice presidents assured me that communication wasn't an issue, instead pointing to problems with adoption and execution.

Before the conference, I suspected a disconnect between the C-suite and company leaders. My intention in Miami wasn't to embarrass senior leadership or prove a point, but to sincerely assess the collective viewpoint. There was a palpable sigh of relief when I asked those in attendance to pause, look around, and notice that everyone had raised their hand. Regardless of what those at the top believed, these hands were irrefutable evidence.

The truth is that many cannot fix the issues preventing them from growing as communicators because they're painfully unaware they even exist. What they believe about their communication effectiveness doesn't always match reality. There's often a significant divide between how well leaders think they communicate and how well others understand them. Overcoming this gap is challenging but crucial because leaders are in the business of communicating. Whether interacting with individuals, teams, or entire organizations, a significant part of the leader's day revolves around talking. As such, we must recognize:

- Talking at people differs greatly from delivering a clear, engaging, relevant message that connects and resonates with them.
- Effective communication is about forming a connection, not just broadcasting information. It's about understanding your audience, recognizing their challenges, and connecting with them on a level that transcends superficial chatter.

The misunderstanding around the effectiveness of communication is called the perception fallacy. Many leaders believe they're excellent communicators because their schedule is packed with meetings and discussions. However, you discover a different story when you ask team members further down the chain of command. The essence of transformative leadership lies in bridging this perceptual divide, fostering genuine connections, and developing a communication style that resonates with every tier of the organizational ladder.

The Power of Story

In December 1994, archaeologists analyzed over 1,000 Paleolithic-era cave paintings at the Chauvet-Pont-d'Arc Cave in France. Thirty-two thousand years earlier, the Aurignacian people documented their existence on these walls using simple depictions of cave lions, bears, and mammoths. While the connection between cave drawings and effective communication may seem like a stretch, they're linked by the ability to captivate, influence, and engage their respective audiences. Although beautiful, these depictions of the hunter-gatherer life were not the product of some deep need for creative expression. Instead, the art on these frigid limestone walls speaks to a universal desire to communicate stories, record experiences, and protect cultural legacies.[5]

Transformational leaders use the art of storytelling to inspire people, shape the future, and ensure continuity, much like ancient humans used cave drawings to pass wisdom between generations. Presidents John F. Kennedy and Ronald Reagan, along with civil rights leader Martin Luther King Jr., are examples of leaders who understood the power of using stories to illustrate values, spread ideas, and establish shared purpose. They were experts in timing their anecdotes for maximum connection; this allowed them to relate to audiences on an emotional level and lent credibility to their arguments.

Neuroscience confirms that storytelling is compelling because it helps us connect with characters, envision scenarios, and retain critical details.[6] In contrast to facts and figures, stories trigger a process in the brain called neural coupling, creating such a strong emotional connection that the listener feels the story is personally addressed to them. But storytelling is more than just sharing stories; it's knowing and caring about your audience. Those who aspire to be influential leaders must understand the importance of active listening, empathy, and creating a space for genuine interaction.

Leaders who use storytelling to inspire stand out because people crave meaningful connections. By sharing personal stories that move the hearts and minds of their audience, leaders transcend conventional notions of authority and become approachable mentors and guides.

Imperatives: Your Communication Toolbox

Hopefully, you see the value of strengthening your communication skills. The ability to communicate effectively is a game-changer for any leader, and you don't need to be a professional speaker to get your message across; you need to commit yourself to improving, progressing, and helping others. Effective communication positively impacts every aspect of life, making it a powerful tool for transformational leaders. No matter where you are now, the ability to communicate has the potential to become your greatest strength—your superpower.

Here are five imperatives to start improving your communication as a leader.

Imperative 1: Overcommunicate

In today's fast-paced world, we're all juggling a lot. There's a constant buzz of distractions, from emails and texts to urgent tasks that suddenly pop up. Over-communicating is better than under-communicating, especially when the message is crucial. Each time you repeat the message, you boost the chances of it being heard, understood, and remembered. It's simple yet effective. Over time, this practice of over-communication will help get your message across and foster a culture of open communication, making it easier to lead and collaborate.

Imperative 2: Collect and Share Relevant Stories

Find stories that strengthen your message, collect them, and share them when you feel they'll make the most significant impact. These could be based on personal experiences, historical events, or allegorical tales. Whether during a team meeting, a casual conversation, or a formal presentation, a relevant story can magnify the impact of your message, making it both memorable and relatable. Sharing stories results in a deeper understanding and a shared sense of purpose. Over time, as you hone this skill, you'll notice a more engaged audience. Start collecting stories and embrace the power of storytelling to enhance your communication and leadership.

Imperative 3: Adapt Your Style

People are diverse, and so is how they understand and process information. That's why it's essential to tweak your communication based on who you're speaking with. Adapting your style isn't about changing your message; it's about delivering it in a way that resonates with your audience. For example, if you're explaining a new process to your team, you might draw a flowchart for the visual learners, discuss the topic in detail for the verbal learners, and run a mock scenario for those who learn by doing. Mixing up things lets you meet people where they are, making it easier for them to grasp the point. This small effort can go a long way in helping you become a more effective and appreciated leader.

Imperative 4: Be Clear and Concise

The key to effective communication is keeping things simple and straight to the point. Avoid complex terms that might confuse people and stick to clear language everyone understands. You aim to share information and add value, not impress people with big words or complex ideas. But even when you think you've nailed your message, it's always good to check. Ask someone you trust for feedback to see if your message comes across as intended. Were there any confusing parts? Anything they misunderstood? And when feedback comes, don't get defensive; embrace it. It's a chance to refine your communication skills and become a better listener.

Imperative 5: Practice Patience

Communicating can sometimes feel like playing a game of telephone where what you say isn't what the listener hears. It can be frustrating, especially when it's important information. But here's where patience becomes your ally. A willingness to repeat your message or explain it differently isn't a sign of weak communication; it's a sign of a patient, emotionally intelligent leader. Think of it like teaching someone to ride a bike; it might take a few tries, a different explanation, or a new approach before they get it. When you show patience, you create a safe environment where your team feels comfortable asking questions and seeking clarification. A small investment of time and patience can yield big dividends in team cohesion, trust, and effectiveness.

The Journey Toward Effective Communication

Like De Beers transformed diamonds from an unnecessary luxury item into a symbol of enduring love and commitment, your leadership narrative has the potential to inspire, catalyze change, and make a lasting impact on the world. Therefore, let your growth as a communicator illuminate the path of those around you, inspiring them to reach their full potential.

Effective communication is not a destination but a continuous journey; every day presents new opportunities to apply, refine, and master the tools outlined in this chapter. Understand that communication is about cultivating a mindset of patience, openness, and curiosity toward how others see the world. As you hone your skills and embrace the power of storytelling, you'll see that the essence of impactful communication is rooted in the respect you show for the voices around you.

Take a moment to reflect on your journey toward transformative leadership and recognize that your ability to communicate doesn't just get your message across—it defines your legacy.

19

Coaching for Success: Growing and Developing Talent

A coach is someone who tells you what you don't want to hear, who has you see what you don't want to see, so you can be who you have always known you could be.

—Tom Landry

ANYONE WHO DEDICATES enough time and effort can become adequate at almost anything. But can you imagine if Tiger Woods had set his sights on being an adequate golfer or if Muhammad Ali's goal was to be good enough at boxing? Thankfully, these men had the talent and drive to become legends.

Since you're reading this book, it's safe to assume that *adequate* and *good enough* are not what you're after, nor should they be. Instead, you're interested in pursuing excellence, but just as Woods had Butch Harmon[1] and Ali had Angelo Dundee,[2] greatness requires more than time—it takes coaching.

Coaching is widely recognized and celebrated where its necessity is unquestionable, including in athletics, the military, emergency response, and more. It baffles me how we recognize the value of coaching, except when it comes to leaders coaching their people. I've watched this deficiency impact organizations worldwide in business, education, and other fields. In each case, there's a notion that

165

ongoing development is best addressed later, at a more opportune time. We both know there's no such thing as the perfect moment.

As a leader, you must prioritize coaching those you lead rather than treating their continuous development as optional. Do you want to achieve sustained excellence? Then it's an absolute must.

The Difference Maker

The difference between highly influential leaders who make an impact and those who sit stagnant is their commitment to coaching. What do I mean by *coaching*? It refers to a leader supporting the development of team members by helping them recognize their full potential, experience continual professional growth, and acquire new skills and strengthen existing ones.[3]

It's defined by a leader seeing the strengths and development areas of those they're responsible for guiding and using that information as a roadmap to help them succeed. This type of coaching runs counter to traditional leadership that leverages a command-and-control model through a framework of vertical hierarchies. While we'll discuss the critical competencies and skills needed to become a more effective coach, it's essential to understand that it all begins with the desire and willingness to commit and serve.

All leaders can coach, but coaching isn't predicated on capability. Instead, it's about willingness. I've met countless people in the sports and business worlds who are capable of greatness if they only put in the effort. Sadly, few ever do. Then there are high achievers who, believing results will be enough, ignore their responsibility to coach those they lead. In time, it becomes evident that their inability to think and behave as anything other than an individual contributor severely hinders their impact. The truth is that coaching is as much about developing the right mindset as it is about acquiring the right skill set. Invest in coaching, and your likelihood of success increases dramatically.

The ability to cultivate and support the development of those you lead is a hallmark of great leadership; coaching is simply an effective mechanism for getting you there. Research paints a compelling narrative of how impactful and widespread the focus on coaching is. David E. Gray, professor of leadership and organizational behavior at the University of Greenwich, found that more than 59% of large companies operate coaching programs, and 70% cite coaching as essential to leadership development.[4]

According to a peer-reviewed study by Dr. Steven J. Stowell, co-founder of the Center for Management and Organization Effectiveness, coaching leadership presents four primary components: direction, development, accountability, and relationships.[5]

Let's examine and add to each of these components:

1. **Direction**
   - **Desired Destination:** Effective coaching leadership begins with identifying a desired destination. Leaders must articulate and define the path forward.
   - **Guidance:** Leaders must constantly guide team members toward the key objectives.
   - **Decision-Making:** Leaders must foster good decision-making by helping team members weigh the pros and cons and supporting them in making well-informed decisions.
   - **Communicate:** Offering clear and concise communication and feedback is crucial in helping team members grow.
2. **Development**
   - **Enhance Skills:** Leaders must identify each team member's strengths and help them improve areas of weakness through training and mentoring.
   - **Consistent Feedback:** Providing constructive, timely feedback that connects to a team member's core development is crucial.
   - **Empower:** Empowering team members to take on new challenges and responsibilities encourages personal and professional growth.
   - **Create Learning Opportunities:** Create a learning environment where members are encouraged to make mistakes and improve.
3. **Accountability**
   - **Set Expectations:** Setting clear expectations and ensuring team members understand their responsibilities are the cornerstones of accountability.

- **Measure Performance:** Regularly measuring and reviewing performance targets helps maintain transparency and accountability.
- **Responsibility Ownership:** Encourage team members to take ownership of their actions and outcomes.
- **Address Issues:** Addressing performance issues promptly and helping individuals get back on track is also crucial to accountability.

4. Relationships
   - **Build Trust:** Building a trusting and respectful relationship is crucial for creating a positive coaching environment.
   - **Communicate Openly:** Establishing open communication channels helps build solid relationships. Team members should feel comfortable discussing issues and sharing feedback.
   - **Resolve Conflict:** Leaders should be adept at identifying and resolving conflicts to strengthen coaching relationships and promote a positive environment.
   - **Recognize Effort:** Recognizing and appreciating the efforts and achievements of team members play a significant role in building strong relationships.

These four components interrelate and overlap in practice, creating a practical coaching framework that allows leaders to foster a high-performing, engaging, and collaborative team environment.

Confronting Resistance

As I said in the first chapter, leadership is a tremendous honor and a heavy burden. Part of this burden stems from the unrealistic expectation that we simultaneously focus our time and energy in multiple directions. As such, leaders have countless excuses for not investing their time, effort, and resources into coaching, with the most popular being that they have more pressing issues.

Stephen Covey captured this when he warned, "The noise of the urgent creates the illusion of importance." I have used this quote for over a decade to illustrate that not everything that seems urgent is. The skill lies in discerning and prioritizing actions most likely to produce optimal outcomes.

At a time when everything is labeled urgent, it becomes imperative for leaders to deliberately slow down, evaluate, and determine what truly warrants immediate attention.

Despite these insights, resistance to coaching persists. The three main excuses for this resistance can be identified, along with their underlying issues and strategies to overcome them. By addressing these excuses, leaders can realign their focus and better understand the importance of coaching in effective leadership.

1. **Time Excuse:** "I simply don't have the time. Perhaps I'll get to it later."
   - **Underlying Issue:** This excuse stems from a lack of prioritization or understanding of the long-term benefits. It can also result from poor time management or an overly hectic schedule.
   - **Overcoming the Excuse:** Leaders can overcome this barrier by:
     o Understanding the value of coaching and its long-term benefits.
     o Prioritizing coaching as a crucial part of their role.
     o Managing time more effectively to create space for coaching.
     o Setting aside dedicated time for coaching interactions, making it a regular part of the schedule.
2. **Knowledge Gap:** "More pressing matters require my attention."
   - **Underlying Issue:** Leaders might perceive other matters as more urgent, especially in a crisis or high-pressure situation. This excuse reflects a reactive rather than proactive leadership approach.
   - **Overcoming the Excuse:** To address this, leaders might:
     o Understand that coaching can help build a more self-reliant, skilled, and motivated team, which will alleviate the pressing issues over time.
     o Learn to balance immediate concerns with long-term development.
     o Delegate specific responsibilities to trusted team members to free up time for coaching and addressing other crucial matters.

3. **Disillusion Factor:** "I hold regular team meetings, which serve as coaching."

    ■ **Underlying Issue:** This excuse reflects a misunderstanding of what coaching entails. Regular team meetings are essential for communication, but they do not replace the personalized, developmental, and empowering aspects of coaching.

    ■ **Overcoming the Excuse:** To overcome this excuse, leaders can:
       o Educate themselves on the essence and benefits of coaching.
       o Start incorporating coaching elements into interactions with team members, such as personalized feedback, goal setting, and developmental conversations.
       o Dedicate time for consistent one-on-one coaching sessions to address individual needs and foster personal and professional growth.

These excuses can be dismantled and overcome with a better understanding of the importance of coaching, improved time management, and a willingness to adjust priorities to include coaching as a fundamental aspect of leadership. Someone will always try to persuade you that there are more important things than coaching, but you must be steadfast in confronting and overcoming that resistance.

Transformational leaders are considered larger-than-life with the ability to inspire large groups. While there may be some validity to this, what a leader does behind the scenes, such as engaging in regular one-on-one interactions, enables them to make a significant impact.

The Four Coaching Imperatives

Now that we've established its significance let's discuss the four coaching imperatives. These four principles—consistency, individualization, formality, informality—will help you gain clarity as a leader and make the most of your coaching.

Consistency

There's a significant difference between doing something occasionally and doing it consistently. Coaching is like fitness in that your level of consistency will largely determine your results.

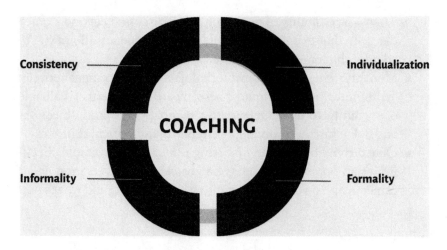

Figure 19.1   The Four Coaching Imperatives.

I recently spent a week at a client's headquarters for its annual strategic planning meeting. About six months before this meeting, the executive team and HR announced that coaching would be a priority for all leaders and managers. On the day of the meeting, they were unhappy with the results. At the start of an all-day session, I asked the five leaders at my table how their coaching was going. I received a blank stare. When a leader broke the awkward silence, he admitted to meeting with his direct reports once. Another leader explained that she hadn't had time to devote to her seven direct reports and would begin working on it next month. The other three leaders at the table echoed similar sentiments. These five leaders had one coaching session with each of their direct reports in the six months since the initiative launched. I soon learned it wasn't just the leaders at my table; all 35 attendees had similar stories. How can an initiative implemented because of poor employee engagement not be prioritized?

There's no right or wrong cadence for coaching; determine what has the most significant impact and remain consistent. I prefer weekly, monthly, or quarterly, and have found most leaders respond well to this model.

- **Weekly:** Brief yet meaningful interactions lasting no more than 5 to 10 minutes. This is an excellent opportunity to discuss how to make progress toward weekly objectives and significant projects.

There's a possibility of not much being discussed beyond a quick check-in, but even that's valuable. This frequency allows you to address challenges as they arise.

- **Monthly:** This more extensive dialogue typically ranges between 30 minutes and an hour. These meetings present a valuable opportunity to evaluate progress reports, goals, and objectives and delve into an individual's strengths and critical skill sets.
- **Quarterly:** The quarterly meeting is more than a simple check-in; it's an opportunity to have a productive conversation about career goals and delve deeper into what's working and what's not.

Individualization

Coaching must be tailored to the individual because cookie-cutter coaching doesn't work. What works for one team member may not work for another. Leaders mustn't fall into the trap of going through the motions and spending time with people to say they did it, even if it had little impact.

This is where understanding your target audience and doing whatever it takes to connect personally will be useful. You'll never connect if you don't know your people. The inability to relate to people will always get in the way of building trust and customizing your coaching.

Asking team members how they prefer to be recognized for a job well done, how they learn and retain information, and if there's anything you can do differently are all simple but incredibly effective methods for personalizing your coaching. You may get little to no information the first few times you ask these questions, but if you keep at it, you might be surprised at what you learn. Although it may seem obvious, a shockingly low percentage of leaders take the time to ask their teams straightforward questions. Once you know, each subsequent interaction is more efficient and effective.

Formality

There is a common misconception about coaching: every coaching interaction will be the same regarding how it is delivered and what it entails for those coached. All great coaches undoubtedly engage in a more formal coaching mode, wherein sessions are planned and adhere to the allotted time. Leaders who want to coach effectively must practice as their favorite sports team does before a big game.

The formal part of coaching should include a detailed outline of the topics to be covered, a detailed agenda, and all necessary resources and instructions in advance. There is more to the formal side of coaching than just sticking to a schedule. It may also involve role-playing an important aspect of their job or going through a live walk-through. Although the specifics of a coaching session will vary greatly depending on several factors, the formal cadence should be spelled out in advance to avoid any confusion or misunderstandings.

Informality

The informal exists apart from the formal. Without diminishing the value of the other elements, which are all important, this one has the greatest potential for impact. The informal aspect of coaching is particularly effective because it takes place at the moment and is tied to actual performance at work.

It could mean spending 10 minutes reviewing aspects of a team member's client presentation immediately rather than waiting for your meeting. It could also mean "management by wandering around," which is catching people doing the right thing and providing immediate recognition to reinforce the behavior.

All four coaching imperatives are interconnected and mutually reinforce one another to some degree. However, the informal aspect presents the most significant potential for promoting knowledge transfer and applying skills or competencies to daily duties. Why is this so important? What good is it to meet and coach your people if they leave those meetings without putting what was discussed and reviewed into practice? Ultimately, the purpose of coaching extends beyond dedicating time to support team members; it's also to facilitate personal growth, development, and self-improvement while simultaneously generating tangible outcomes with significant impact.

Becoming a Coaching Leader

Becoming a coaching leader requires a blend of personal development, skill-building, and establishing a supportive environment for your team. Here are five action items and best practices to start with:

1. **Develop Core Coaching Skills:**
   - **Active Listening:** Engage in active listening, which involves hearing the words and understanding the intentions behind them.
   - **Effective Questioning:** Ask empowering and probing questions that challenge your team and promote self-reflection.
   - **Feedback:** Practice giving concise, constructive feedback that's clear, specific, and focused on growth.
2. **Establish Comfortability:** Build trust with your team by being authentic, open, and respectful. Ensure a psychologically safe environment where individuals feel comfortable sharing ideas, asking questions, and admitting mistakes.
3. **Create Individual Development Plans:** Collaborate with team members to identify personal and professional goals. Design personalized coaching plans to help them achieve these goals while aligning with larger objectives connected to their day-to-day responsibilities.
4. **Promote Continuous Learning and Reflection:** Encourage a culture of continuous learning and development, share resources, hold regular training sessions, and provide opportunities for skill-building. Debrief after projects or notable events to reflect on successes, challenges, and key learnings.
5. **Measure and Celebrate Progress:** Set measurable objectives and key results to track progress. Celebrate achievements and progress toward goals, no matter how small. Recognition and celebration foster a positive culture and excitement for continual growth.

Coaching focuses on helping others learn and is centered on asking questions instead of giving instructions—sparking reflection instead of providing guidelines. Becoming a coaching leader is a journey that requires a strong commitment to personal growth and your team's success. By fostering a supportive environment and honing your coaching skills, you'll be well on your way to embodying the qualities needed to make a lasting difference.

20

Empowering Others to Lead and Make an Impact

Leaders don't create followers; they create more leaders.

—Tom Peters

In this book, we've touched on what makes a leader great. Yet, it's important to note that what allows one leader to guide their team toward a brighter future might lead another down a different path. It's like two coaches using the same game plan, but one ends in a touchdown and the other a field goal. While every transformational leader is unique in their skills, how they think, and what they value, they all share one key trait: the ability to create more leaders.

The support teams surrounding a leader, like skilled managers, assistants, and administrators, play a huge role in their success. Any organization, whether a business, sports team, or school, needs strong leaders and capable managers to thrive. The beauty of outstanding leadership lies in building a culture where everyone supports and uplifts one another, regardless of their jobs. It's not about titles or climbing the ladder, but fostering a mindset where everyone is encouraged to take ownership and help those around them grow.

This reminds me of a conversation I had with the CEO of a prestigious healthcare network. When asked to describe what he looks for in those he hires, he quickly responded, "Don't tell me everything you've done or accomplished. Give me examples of how you have helped others grow."

True leaders who make a lasting difference and transform organizations go beyond excelling in their roles and achieving impressive results quarter after quarter. Outward success isn't the only thing driving them; there's something more profound. They can set their ego aside and focus on the bigger picture: nurturing and developing new leaders from within the teams. These are men and women driven to see others grow, succeed, and lead.

Instilling Ownership

Do you live in Tennessee? Are you a die-hard NFL fan? If you answered "no" to both questions, it's unlikely that you've watched many Tennessee Titans games or know much about the team's former head coach, Mike Vrabel. Why would you? They're not in a primary market like New York, Boston, Chicago, or Los Angeles, and they've never won a Super Bowl. Still, since taking over as head coach in 2018, Vrabel's leadership has given a glimpse into the franchise's potential.

Coach Vrabel knows the NFL inside and out, not just from the sidelines but from his time on the field. Speaking as a former player, it's evident that his empathy for players allows him to connect better than almost any other coach in the league. Yet, his most significant leadership moment had nothing to do with a player; instead, it centered on an assistant coach.

During a preseason game leading up to the 2023 season, he did something that stunned the football world and left us all in awe. Recognizing the ambition of assistant coach Terrell Williams, Vrabel stepped aside to let him take over the full scope of head coaching operations against the Chicago Bears. The choice to hand over the metaphorical whistle and clipboard from Thursday afternoon until after the game on Saturday wasn't just a simple gesture; it was entrusting decision-making, strategy, and the team's morale to someone else.

Why is this so remarkable? Sure, it helped build Williams's resume, but it also taught coaches and leaders worldwide an invaluable lesson: trust and believe in your team. After the shock began to subside, praise for the decision began; ESPN's Ryan Clark tweeted, "Mike Vrabel gets it, and not only that is empowering his people. Love this! Well done, Vrabs."[1]

Coach Vrabel highlighted the importance of shared ownership and teamwork by giving someone else the stage. Leading isn't always about being in the spotlight. Sometimes, it's about giving others the chance to shine, letting them see the world through new eyes. When that assistant resumed his regular duties, he likely saw things differently. Leadership, after all, is about perspective, and sometimes a shift in viewpoint is all it takes to change a life.

Putting faith in those around you, even if they don't carry the leadership label, communicates their value and instills a sense of loyalty, respect, and ownership in them. Before the game, Coach Williams explained, "What you don't see is what he . . . does for us as coaches and our families. I'll do anything for Mike Vrabel . . . because I know [he] cares for my family. And trust me, for a guy like me, that means a whole hell of a lot."[2]

Invite Others Along for the Journey

Leaders have traditionally gathered in boardrooms to deliberate, debate, and make critical decisions. This longtime practice has become obsolete in a hyper-connected world that demands real-time responses.

Many experienced leaders struggle to make this change, especially those accustomed to doing things a certain way. Still, the effort is entirely worthwhile; we must avoid promoting internal silos by hiding leadership behind closed doors while commanding those impacted most to remain at their desks. Instead, let's invite the rank-and-file into the decision-making process early on. I'm not suggesting that everyone in your organization needs to be involved, but start soliciting feedback, insight, and ideas from a broad cross-section of employees by asking what they'd do if they were in charge. Who knows—maybe they will be one day.

Your initial instinct may be to think of ways this could backfire. Invite your organization's legal team to do this exercise with you, and watch as that list expands exponentially. Soon, you'll have pages of excuses on why you shouldn't do it, including the likelihood it turns into a whining session or provides ammunition for your critics.

These certainly have merit—after all, there's risk involved in everything worthwhile—but these are the same reasons companies fear social media and are quick to block anyone they believe is critical of them. But, just as social media has demonstrated, there is power in transparency—people no longer accept the false narrative of perfection peddled by corporate brands since the early 1950s. Now, people want—or rather, they demand—sincerity and honesty. When done correctly, the transformative effects of inviting employees into the process can be monumental, but, like posting on social media, it's not a one-time thing.

I've witnessed the incredible transformative power of inclusive decision-making on workplace culture and morale firsthand; it's truly eye-opening. For it to work, decision-makers must solicit feedback from those who will roll up their sleeves and implement the vision. While this practice fosters a healthier team dynamic, its value lies in cultivating a trusted group of individuals whose candid insights you can rely on. Embrace this, and in time, you'll notice two extraordinary shifts:

1. The source of your next groundbreaking idea becomes boundless. You never know—the quietest voice in the room might surprise you with game-changing insight. This approach rewards outside-the-box thinking and seeds a culture where the spotlight shines based on the merit of ideas, not the position of those voicing them.
2. A strong sense of ownership emerges, reshaping how individuals connect with their work and daily responsibilities. The disengagement gap starts to be bridged when team members see that their insights and opinions have power.

Never lose sight of this fact: the more individuals feel that their contributions are valued and that the doors of opportunity are open, the more dedicated they become to seeing it through. Another concern many leaders have involves the ramifications of choosing one team member's idea over another's. They fail to recognize that it isn't the implementation of ideas that contributes to a team member's feelings of worth and value, but having an opportunity to share their thoughts and engage in meaningful discussions.

Write Your Lottery Ticket

In 1979, behavioral economist Daniel Kahneman conducted research that resulted in him being awarded the Nobel Memorial Prize in Economics in 2002. His research, which laid the foundation for Prospect Theory, studied whether participants were more committed to the lottery tickets they'd selected than those randomly assigned. The key finding was that individuals demanded at least five times more money to sell back their personalized tickets, indicating a significant increase in perceived value and commitment when they had the autonomy to make their own choices.[3]

This concept involves leaders inviting those they lead into the decision-making process. Allowing team members to "write their own lottery ticket," a phrase coined by McKinsey & Company, empowers them to take ownership and meaningfully contribute to the broader narrative. This approach fosters commitment, ownership, and engagement toward organizational objectives.[4]

What does that look like in the real world? Edward Neville Isdell became the CEO of Coca-Cola in 2004, during a period of notable downturn. He recognized the need for a comprehensive turnaround strategy but chose an unconventional development method. Instead of confining the strategic planning to the executive suite, Isdell invited the top 150 employees to co-create the pathway forward.

This initiative was an exercise in cultivating ownership and commitment. Isdell's approach allowed these employees to "write their own lottery ticket" by having a significant say in the direction of one of the most iconic companies in history. Soon, it cascaded down through the organization via smaller working meetings, where employees examined the implications of the strategy for their respective departments, personalizing the broader organizational narrative.

The impact of this inclusive strategy was profound. In two years, Coca-Cola transitioned from freefall to realizing a 20% return. The company also witnessed a 25% reduction in staff turnover and substantial upticks in employee engagement. Leaders benefit from a stronger sense of ownership by broadening the spectrum of involvement in the decision-making process. Having had a say in the organizational objectives, Cocoa-Cola employees were more likely to be committed to the outcomes, much like the individuals in the lottery experiment who valued their personally chosen numbers significantly more.[5]

The effectiveness of this approach highlights the importance of involving team members in the decision-making process to cultivate a greater sense of commitment and engagement, driving greater organizational success.

The Power of Dreams

Recently, I spent the week at an off-site retreat with a large group of leaders from Bernards. The California-based company, an industry leader in commercial building and construction management, had experienced steady growth over the years, but the pace of internal change had recently increased exponentially. At the retreat, the team spent their days focused on growing as leaders and crafting the organization's strategy.

I had already worked with Bernards for nearly a year, but there was something magical about taking time to work on the business rather than in it. But the real magic happened each night during dinner when we conducted team-building exercises.

One evening, we asked them to share a personal dream, goal, or aspiration with the group. Given their history working together, you might assume these 50 leaders couldn't learn anything new about one another—but you'd be wrong. Some initially tried glossing over the personal aspect of the assignment, but I urged them to dig deep and get personal. Once the first few opened up, something incredible happened: the more they spoke about their hopes, dreams, and ambitions, the more others wanted to share. I watched the group learn more about those they thought they knew; it was surreal and fulfilling.

The following evening, during our final dinner, a leader gave a heartfelt toast and sat back down. Not even 10 seconds later, another stood up and did the same thing, except she shared something personal. After she finished, a third leader gave an inspiring account of what it meant to work at Bernards and shared his renewed dedication to the team.

Why am I sharing this? Unlike the previous night, I hadn't asked the group to do this. Still, all 50 leaders gave an unrehearsed, heartfelt toast. What began as a team-building exercise the night before organically grew into a transformative experience. Working with someone for a decade can create the illusion of familiarity, but genuinely knowing a person requires work—it requires learning their passions, values, hopes, and dreams.

Fostering a culture where individuals feel comfortable sharing their true selves is fundamental to them effecting change where they are. Promoting a reflective environment where people can explore and articulate their values and dreams enhances the likelihood of them taking ownership of their actions and contributing to the team.

PART

VI

Cultivating Team Excellence

21

Building High-Performing Teams

The strength of the team is each individual member. The strength of each member is the team.

—Phil Jackson

TERRELL OWENS'S ATHLETIC ability was undeniable, catching passes that left fans in awe. Still, even though he ranks among the best receivers of all time, started in six Pro Bowls, and led the league in touchdowns in 2001, 2002, and 2006, he was passed over for the Hall of Fame the first two times he was eligible. How can this be? Throughout his career, whispers followed him from team to team. Though he was a talent on the field, in the locker room, his presence was like a storm cloud.

Owens craved recognition and was unapologetic about it. He didn't hesitate to voice his discontent when he felt underappreciated or underpaid; this bothered many in the stands, the locker room, and the sports media. His disputes with teammates and management were aired publicly, and this refusal to place the team's needs first overshadowed his talent. A contractual dispute with the Philadelphia Eagles led to a fallout with management and star quarterback Donovan McNabb.[1] The locker room, once united, began showing cracks. Despite his monumental talent, his inability to foster unity and resolve conflicts maturely cast a long shadow.

His bouncing from team to team told a story of a supremely talented athlete whose inability to lead and be a part of a cohesive unit reduced what could have been a legendary career. Terrell Owens shows us that while talent may win games, teamwork wins championships.

No matter how talented, inspirational, or charismatic a leader is, they will not make a lasting impact if they cannot build and maintain high-performing teams. Football has taught me many life lessons, for which I'm grateful. However, the most valuable is that it requires enduring commitment to build a winning team. Unlike basketball, where a couple of all-star players can turn an average team into champions, football requires that every player do their job for the entire 3 hours and 12 minutes between kickoff and the final whistle.

Rudy. Varsity Blues. Remember the Titans. While there's no shortage of great football movies, my all-time favorite is *Any Given Sunday.* There's a scene in which coach Tony D'Amato, played by Al Pacino, delivers a pre-game speech to his team that explains the parallels between success in life and winning on the gridiron:

> You find out that life is a game of inches, and so is football. Because in either game—life or football—the margin for error is so small. I mean, one half step too late or too early [and] you don't quite make it. A half second too slow or too fast, and you don't catch it. The inches we need are everywhere around us. . .[and] on this team, we fight for that inch. . .because we know when [they] add up all those inches, that's gonna make the difference between winning and losing![2]

An organization's success can be directly traced back to the ability of leadership to build a team that marches in unison. Developing high-performing teams is crucial, and transformational leaders are deliberate in their strategy to increase effectiveness. After all, continual improvement is the key to unlocking collaboration, fostering engagement, and boosting overall productivity. Simple enough? Not at all. Achieving maximum effectiveness is so challenging that leaders must put their team above all else.

Before we move forward, let's define team effectiveness; it encompasses the degree to which a team achieves its specified goals, objectives, and deliverables. When discussing team effectiveness, most people think of team performance. While undeniably important, several factors shape a team's long-term sustainability and well-being. This is reflected in productivity, quality of work, and outcomes underpinned by communication, collaboration, and cohesion among team members.

Effective teams demonstrate adaptability to changing conditions and efficient resource management aligned with organizational objectives. Their innovative nature and problem-solving skills further contribute to their ability to overcome challenges and deliver exceptional results. Moreover, the satisfaction of stakeholders, a thriving culture, and the drive for continuous improvement are pivotal in gauging and enhancing team effectiveness over time, making it a multifaceted attribute of successful team dynamics within and beyond the organizational setting.[3]

A Lesson from the Army

A defining characteristic of high-performing teams is prioritizing collective interests over individual ambitions. When team members put the team first, a strong bond of trust and collaboration forms, significantly enhancing their overall resilience. The U.S. Army has been doing this effectively since being established in 1775. As outlined in the Army's Team Building Techniques Publication, Section 1:14:

> Team members develop accountability focused on the team rather than the individual. This means that team members feel mutually accountable to each other. The team accepts accountability for the results of the team's actions. Team members begin to develop shared competence and shared confidence.[4]

Organizations aiming to cultivate a strong culture built on teamwork must communicate a zero-tolerance policy for behaviors that prioritize personal success over team goals. It's essential to define what's acceptable and what's not early on. Recognizing and appreciating individuals who exhibit desirable traits while addressing behaviors that undermine cohesion is crucial. Establishing clear expectations and developing a system of accountability ensures everyone understands the value placed on teamwork and the principle that team success leads to individual success.

I recently worked with a leading national accounting firm. During my seven weeks there, an executive continually expressed frustration over the lack of trust, collaboration, and teamwork among departments. Although leadership frequently spoke about the company's dedication to teamwork, their words failed to align with reality. In addition, they struggled with equal accountability. Several top performers were frequently late to meetings, displayed a sense of superiority, and alienated teammates. Still, the company took no corrective measures.

This narrative underscores a critical point: talking about teamwork is insufficient if leaders fail to prioritize these values by setting an example and holding everyone accountable for maintaining a collaborative environment. Without this level of commitment from the top, barriers to effective teamwork will persist, leading to poor performance and internal discord.

The Overlooked Component

Being a good teammate is undervalued and often goes unnoticed. Yet, it's the foundation for building and sustaining a strong team. Great teams don't just happen by accident; they require that we put as much effort into learning to be a great teammate as we do in selecting the team's members. It's counterproductive to judge others solely based on perceived actions against the team's interests while self-evaluating based on intent; this dichotomy leads to discontentment and underperformance. If individuals focus on what's best for the team and regularly evaluate how they support their peers, the results will speak for themselves.

Building an effective team comes down to honest communication. For teams to be dynamic, they must also be in sync, meaning transparency and ongoing conversations. This can be as simple as scheduling a monthly meeting where team members answer and discuss two questions about their actions since the previous meeting and ways they can improve before the next one. A few examples include:

- Have my actions helped or hurt the team?
- Where can I add value?
- How have I supported a teammate in overcoming a challenge or achieving a goal?

- Am I open to feedback, and how have I demonstrated this?
- Have I communicated my ideas and concerns in a way that's contributed to the team's objectives, and how can I improve my communication?

These questions prompt introspection on our efficacy as teammates. When leaders weave these questions into their monthly team check-ins, they nurture a culture of continuous improvement. However, this reflective practice is just a stepping-stone toward emphasizing the importance of being a responsible teammate. Your team must reach a consensus on what good teamwork looks like to move the needle. This doesn't require an exhaustive list; pinpoint three core attributes for team members to strive for.

The Bedrock of Great Teams

When it comes to elite teams, trust isn't a passing trend; it's the cornerstone of remarkable achievement and innovation. Without trust, the gears of collaboration seize, the spark of collective brilliance fades away, and mistrust grows. Embarking on the journey of nurturing trust requires patience, intention, and unwavering commitment, even when uncertain. Let's explore the real-world dynamics of trust through the lens of the U.S. Navy SEAL community.

Before earning their trident, Navy SEAL recruits must endure Basic Underwater Demolition/SEAL training (BUD/S). The grueling six-month training has a failure rate of 85% and tests endurance, strength, and determination under some of the harshest conditions imaginable. But it's also a masterclass in the importance of trust and teamwork. The brutal workouts, sleep deprivation, and relentless drills aren't just about molding physical power; they create a crucible of shared adversity, forging bonds among the recruits that last a lifetime. In the cold, dark waters, on the grueling obstacle courses, and during the endless physical training, they find strength in each other. They learn to anticipate each other's movements, cover their backs, and pull one another up from the brink of failure. It's in shared hardship that an unbreakable trust is forged.[5]

The Navy purposely designed this training program to be impossible to complete alone; it calls for a collective effort where success for one is success for all, and failure for one is failure for all. Through these tasks, recruits learn that trust is the currency of survival and success.

The simulated life-and-death scenarios further etch the importance of trust into each recruit's psyche. In the most visceral way imaginable, they understand that their lives and missions hinge on each other. They learn that trust is a two-way street where honest, direct communication is crucial for individual and collective improvement. Above all, SEAL recruits learn that earning trust requires being reliable in all situations, never quitting, and always being there to help.

The essence of BUD/S is to cultivate formidable warriors and instill in them that trust is the bedrock on which a SEAL operates. Because for SEALs, trust isn't just a virtue; it's the difference between life and death.

22

Extreme Accountability Through Established Norms

Professional accountability is a good thing.
Without it, excellence is merely a pipe dream and even average performance
isn't a realistic expectation.

—Leon Ellis

AT THE CORE of transformational leadership lies extreme accountability, a virtue that enhances individual performance and cultivates an environment conducive to collective growth. Instilling this virtue within a team requires establishing and nurturing norms, those unspoken yet clearly understood rules that guide behavior. This chapter delineates the importance of fostering accountability through established norms, paving the way for a thriving culture.

The absence of extreme accountability within a team harms trust, cooperation, and productivity, leading to a gradual deterioration. This fatal flaw reduces a leader's capacity to address problems and take immediate action, resulting in finger-pointing and denial.

Driving accountability is intrinsically tied to leadership, as leaders play a crucial role in establishing and upholding standards. Through their actions, leaders can either demonstrate a commitment to high standards or convey a lack of accountability. Often, organizations invest time and money in developing formal accountability policies and are shocked when things fall apart. The truth is that a leader's daily actions are far more influential in determining accountability than policies ever could be. Leaders who avoid responsibility shift the culture toward the norm of diminished accountability.

Norms lay the groundwork for what's expected from each team member and serve as a behavioral framework within which they operate. Outlining what's acceptable and what isn't reduces ambiguity and better positions them to meet and exceed expectations. This framework is indispensable for nurturing extreme accountability as it promotes a sense of responsibility toward these norms. This shared ethos becomes evident in every action, decision, and interaction.

Leaders who respect and value accountability inspire, influence, and lift those around them. Their ability to show vulnerability and take responsibility challenges others to do the same. Team members feel a sense of psychological safety, allowing them to see mistakes as learning opportunities rather than failures. Established norms create a stable environment and give individuals a reliable standard for evaluating their actions, fostering greater accountability.

Although leadership bears much responsibility, every team member has a role in ensuring a culture of extreme accountability. Regardless of title, position, or pay grade, everyone can promote or undermine accountability among their peers. Ownership of the process shouldn't be restricted by hierarchical dynamics but ingrained as a standard practice. While it may begin with leadership, accountability is everyone's responsibility, from the intern to the executive.

Master Class in Accountability

It was June 11, 1997. The Chicago Bulls were facing the Utah Jazz in the NBA Finals, and the series was tied heading into Game 5. As fans packed the arena, the legendary Michael Jordan sat in the locker room, severely ill with flu-like symptoms. Many later speculated that it might have been food poisoning, but regardless of the cause, the superstar was visibly weakened and dehydrated.

Most players in that condition would have taken the doctor's advice and sat out the game. However, Jordan, being ultra-competitive by nature and knowing his team depended on him, decided to play.

As a team leader, he'd pushed players to perform at their best and fostered excellence as a team norm. That evening, Number 23 demonstrated incredible resilience by playing 44 minutes. He ended up scoring 38 points, grabbing seven rebounds, and dishing out five assists. During a particularly memorable moment after Jordan made a crucial three-point shot, he wrapped his arms around teammate Scottie Pippen to stop himself from collapsing from exhaustion.

The Bulls won the game 90–88 and went on to clinch the series in Game 6, earning Jordan his fifth NBA championship.[1] What do Jordan's actions during this iconic game demonstrate about his leadership?

1. **Dedication:** Jordan was committed to giving his best to the team despite his physical condition. This dedication showcased his intense drive and that he understood his role on the team.
2. **Following Norms:** Under Jordan, the Bulls had established a norm predicated on never making excuses and always putting the team first. His legendary competitiveness and work ethic inspired his teammates to achieve things they never thought possible.
3. **Leading by Example:** Jordan set a standard for his teammates by playing through sickness. His commitment motivated others to push through their challenges.
4. **Accountability:** Jordan knew the importance of the game and didn't want to let down his teammates, coaches, and fans. Instead of using his illness as an excuse, he chose to be accountable to himself and his team.

Michael Jordan's "Flu Game" is a testament to incredible leadership and accountability, highlighting how one individual's determination can inspire an entire team to greatness.

The Damaging Consequences

Accountability isn't a trivial notion casually mentioned and subsequently disregarded; instead, it serves as the core basis of any thriving organization or team. In its absence, aspirations for excellence and the construction of high-performance benchmarks are reduced to mere wishful thinking. The first symptoms of deterioration, such as missed objectives and declining quality, appear when accountability fades. However, that is only the tip of the iceberg.

The negative consequences of a lack of accountability can be severe and multifaceted, impacting various aspects of organizational health and performance; they include increased stress, credibility loss, decreased work quality, a higher probability of legal and ethical violations, lower morale, and many more.

With such high stakes, it's shocking that 82% of managers say they have either limited or no ability to hold others accountable, and 91% of employees believe their company's top leadership development need is holding others accountable. The performance review process is the most potent accountability mechanism teams and organizations have. Still, a Gallup survey reveals that 26% of employees only receive feedback once annually, and only 14% feel their performance is managed in a way that motivates them. Even more alarming, only 21% of team members feel their performance metrics are within their control, and 70% say managers aren't objective in evaluating them.[2]

So, it shouldn't be surprising that 69% of employees feel they're not living up to their full potential. Engagement plummets when people feel powerless to change their circumstances, which explains why only 36% of employees say they are engaged at work.[3]

Closing the Gap

Suffering adverse outcomes due to a lack of responsibility is a concept that's been around for ages. Even though it isn't new, and leaders tackle it in their organizations each day, it remains a consistent challenge. The solution isn't emphasizing accountability to team members, but instead establishing core standards and norms that apply equally to everyone on the team. These standards play a pivotal role in regulating accountability within team settings.

Every team has a gap that consists of behaviors that either help the team advance toward its goals or impede it. This is important to recognize. While the factors enhancing a team's performance might differ from one team to another, this foundational principle remains consistent (Figure 22.1).

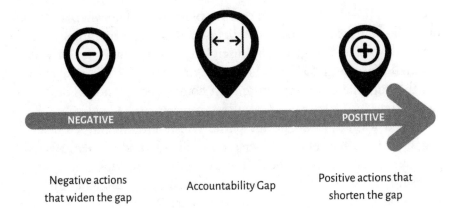

NEGATIVE   POSITIVE

Negative actions
that widen the gap

Accountability Gap

Positive actions that
shorten the gap

Figure 22.1   The Accountability Gap.

A common mistake leaders make is thinking that simply stating the primary objectives for the year or crafting an impactful vision will guarantee the desired outcomes. Setting clear goals is essential, but what distinguishes successful teams is their shared set of norms and beliefs. Accountability issues can become entrenched if we do not regularly discuss expectations and daily standards. As the gap between behaviors and expected standards widens, the challenges to top-notch performance grow.

Bill Walsh, the legendary coach of the San Francisco 49ers, is a prime example of the power of setting clear, unwavering standards. He didn't just tell his players to be accountable; he defined what that meant through his "Standards of Performance." These standards were meticulously crafted, detailing how players should conduct themselves on and off the field.[4] The team struggled when Walsh first took charge of the 49ers in 1979, coming off a 2–14 season. The future looked bleak, and many doubted whether the team could turn things around.

However, Walsh had a vision, and more importantly, a plan. He believed they'd win not by focusing on the result but by emphasizing the process. One of the first things he did was to instill his Standards of Performance. These weren't just about how to throw or catch a football; they covered everything from how players should run routes during practice to how they should conduct themselves in meetings to the attitude and work ethic they should exhibit daily. A well-known example is how Walsh insisted that his players stand up when a coach or a guest entered the room. While it's a seemingly small gesture, it instilled a sense of respect and discipline in the team. Similarly, he required that players and coaches be on time for meetings, underscoring the importance of respecting their commitments and valuing the team's time.

But it wasn't just about discipline; Walsh also emphasized teaching, ensuring every player understood their role and felt empowered to make decisions on the field. This was groundbreaking at the time and shifted the focus from raw talent to intelligence, preparation, and execution—what we now refer to as a player's football IQ.

The results spoke for themselves. Within three years, the 49ers went from being one of the weakest teams in the NFL to Super Bowl champions. Critics at the time attributed his success to luck, but Walsh understood that "luck" was just an excuse used by those unwilling to put in the work. Under Walsh's leadership and commitment to the Standards of Performance, the team would win two more Super Bowls in the 1980s.[5]

Bill Walsh demonstrates that setting and adhering to high standards can lead to success. It wasn't just about talent or strategy but a consistent and holistic approach to excellence, where every action, no matter how minor, was done with intention and purpose. Leaders looking to bridge the standards gap could learn a lot from Walsh's unwavering commitment to his vision and rigorous implementation of standards at every level of the organization.

Beyond Performance: Setting Clear Expectations

Team excellence starts with the hunger and drive to instill clear expectations and standards and the ability never to forget what they are. This can't be lip service or used to fill an upcoming meeting. Creating clear expectations comes down to the daily norms and standards that we demand of everyone and the individual expectations that align with team objectives. It's incredible how people have worked at an organization for over a decade, and still, their understanding of what's expected of them differs from their leader's actual expectations. This is because expectations change and evolve.

Providing clear expectations goes far beyond merely setting a standard of performance. It encompasses every aspect of team conduct, from the overarching objectives to the minutiae of daily interactions and tasks. By being explicit about what is expected, leaders offer their teams a roadmap to success where everyone is aligned, understands their role, and can operate with a shared sense of purpose.

1. **Clear Understanding of the Objectives:** It's not enough for a leader to know the endgame; every team member should also understand what the organization aims to achieve. When everyone is clear on the objectives, it fosters a unified direction. People can more easily prioritize tasks, collaborate effectively, and understand how their contributions fit the bigger picture.

2. **Mapping Out Team Conduct:** Clear expectations extend beyond goals and performance metrics. How a team conducts itself daily, from practicing skills to attending meetings, is equally vital. This involves setting standards for how team members interact, communicate, and behave in their core roles and peripheral activities. Such standards create a cohesive and harmonious work environment where everyone knows the rules of engagement.

3. **Participation and Engagement:** Setting expectations around participation ensures everyone feels involved and invested. Whether it's a brainstorming session or a routine status update, when team members know their active engagement is expected, they are more likely to come prepared, offer insights, and participate actively in discussions.

The power of clear expectations can be seen in Google's rise as one of the world's most influential tech companies. Google's success isn't solely based on its innovative products but is also deeply rooted in its culture and clear expectations. From the outset, Google founders Larry Page and Sergey Brin established a clear mission: "To organize the world's information and make it universally accessible and useful."

This wasn't just a lofty goal; it provided a clear direction for all Googlers (as Google employees are known). Every product or service Google develops furthers this mission.[6]

But Google's expectations didn't stop at the company's overarching objectives.

Google's famous "Ten things we know to be true" is a foundation for how the company approaches product development, placing the user first and focusing on long-term value over short-term gains.

Furthermore, Google emphasizes an open culture in which every Googler is encouraged to bring their ideas to the table, irrespective of hierarchy. This ethos is evident in the company's famed TGIF (Thank God It's Friday) meetings, where employees across all levels ask leaders questions. This promotes active engagement and underscores the expectation that everyone has a valued voice, regardless of rank.

Finally, Google's clear expectations extend to its famed "20% time" policy, where engineers are encouraged to spend 20% of their time working on personal projects that they believe will benefit the company. This policy fosters innovation and communicates that Google values creativity, autonomy, and forward-thinking. Google's success highlights the multifaceted nature of setting clear expectations. It's not just about performance or a single objective but creating a holistic framework that guides everything from mission-critical decisions to daily team interactions. By ensuring everyone is on the same page, leaders can cultivate teams that are productive, engaged, innovative, and aligned with the company's broader vision.

The role of a leader in uniting the team around norms, standards, and extreme accountability is an easy concept to understand but challenging to master. As American management theorist Peter Drucker said, "The leaders who work most effectively . . . never say 'I.' And that's not because they have trained themselves not to . . .[it's because] they don't think 'I.' They think 'we.' They think 'team.' They understand their job to be to make the team function."[7]

23

The Art of Cultivating Resilience and Grit

Grit is passion and perseverance for very long-term goals.
Grit is having stamina. Grit is sticking with your future, day-in, day-out.
Not just for the week, not just for the month, but for years.
And working really hard to make that future a reality.
Grit is living life like it's a marathon, not a sprint.

—Dr. Angela Lee Duckworth

LEADERSHIP IS FAR from a straightforward journey. While it's tempting to fixate on the perks, recognition, and prestige that accompany leadership roles, doing so overshadows an underlying responsibility: steering teams through storms of adversity. But how can we inspire greatness, maintain focus, and champion progress when the world is spinning out of control?

Take a step back to 2019. Globally, we navigated challenges like climate change, political upheavals, and societal shifts. Yes, these issues were significant, but they were hurdles we'd encountered. Then, 2020 marked a seismic shift. The outbreak of the Covid-19 pandemic disrupted the world's rhythm and made even the familiar foreign. Leaders worldwide found themselves at a crossroads, facing the daunting task of crafting responses to an ever-evolving crisis, the repercussions of which resonated far beyond national borders.

The truth is that 2020 was a year of profound disarray. It was humanity's reckoning, akin to a disoriented child lost in the forest. Leaders were thrust into the spotlight, grappling with the pivotal question, "What's our next move?" Amid economic strife, health concerns, and societal breakdown, leadership became more challenging than ever. Is there a playbook for such times? A universal response to navigate such uncharted territories? The reality is that there was no singular correct answer, and leaders were often charting paths with incomplete maps.

So, why revisit a period of such global distress, anxiety, and unease? The simple answer is that transformational leaders clung to hope against the tide of uncertainties, guiding their teams through consecutive challenges and emerging fortified. However, the crisis also exposed leaders who, rather than being pillars of strength, exacerbated their team's hardships and struggles.

The inescapable truth, while complex and uncomfortable, is that crises are inevitable. While future challenges may not mirror the global scale of a pandemic, periods of turbulence await. As such, leaders must prepare by fostering resilience and honing grit; only then can they ensure those they're responsible for remain safe during the storm.

The Starting Point

To truly master resilience, it's essential to anchor ourselves in three foundational truths:

1. There will always be challenges and adversity; it's just a matter of when.
2. Resilience isn't measured by the size of the challenge, but by our response.
3. While the scope and scale may vary, adversity is a universal experience.

An honest self-evaluation of our reactions to adversity is central to overcoming hardship. Our interpretation of setbacks, failures, and navigating the proverbial shark-infested waters influences our reactions and responses.

Transformational leaders recognize adversity as an opportunity for growth. The complexity of a challenge does not paralyze them; they see multifaceted solutions and emerge from each struggle a little stronger. We must embody this attitude as leaders because our credibility suffers if our resolve wavers during crises.

This isn't a call to wear rose-colored glasses in the face of adversity. Instead, it's a reminder to approach challenges with a mindset of possibility and growth. Such a perspective fortifies our resilience and instills a sense of control over outcomes. Conversely, leaders overwhelmed by challenges often feel trapped, viewing their environment as adversarial. This perceived loss of agency impedes our capacity to chart a proactive course forward, sidelining our most potent tool for progress.

How pivotal is this sense of control? According to experts from the University of Florida, individuals who feel in control of their circumstances rather than controlled by them see improvements in nearly all performance metrics.[1]

This mindset benefits the leader and is integral to improving team performance. Why? A composed leader can frame setbacks as growth opportunities and set a positive example for their team.

The Power of Inspiring Hope

Transformational leaders can spark hope in those around them. This unique strength comes from their willingness to face stark realities while lifting spirits and fostering a powerful sense of hope. As I discussed in the first few chapters, many of history's most renowned leaders achieved the impossible due to their talent for inspiring people and sustaining hope.

But instilling hope isn't just a nice-to-have; it's essential for nurturing perseverance and grit within teams and organizations. Angela Duckworth's seminal book *Grit* delineates a triad for cultivating hope: a growth mindset, optimistic self-talk, and relentless perseverance over adversity. She suggests selecting one of these elements and reflecting on how best to grow within that area. This simple method offers a potent blueprint for leaders to amplify reservoirs of hope for themselves and their teams.

At the heart of the growth mindset lies the belief that our capabilities—intelligence, talent, or a combination of the two—aren't static. They can be honed and enhanced with time and effort. Moreover, by consciously choosing optimistic self-talk, especially during turbulent times, we equip ourselves to respond proactively, driving positive change. Such self-talk is not about being unrealistically optimistic, but about constructive reinforcement. An example is a healthcare insurance firm where team members vocalized their commitment to crucial objectives by writing a sentence articulating how their actions would help them achieve critical goals. Such exercises are powerful because they clarify individual responsibilities and create an atmosphere where the emphasis remains on solutions, even when challenges mount.

Perseverance, the third leg of Duckworth's triad, helps build a resilient spirit. Each time a team overcomes an obstacle or achieves a goal, it's not just a win for that moment but a reminder of their collective strength. We must use these moments to celebrate the team's unity, collaboration, and power. And as leaders, when the next challenge comes, remind the team of their past triumphs, reinforcing their ability to rise above once again.[2]

For transformational leaders, the mission is clear: foster hope consistently, in good times and bad. Because with a wellspring of hope comes a heightened resolve to journey toward a brighter, boundless future.

Developing an Elite Mindset

"The only easy day was yesterday." This is a well-known saying within the Navy SEAL community. While simple, its implications run deep, encapsulating the ethos, challenges, and resilient mindset that SEALs must embody. But you don't have to join one of the world's most elite fighting forces to embrace this philosophy.

For example, take the story of Jessica Watson, the young Australian sailor who set out to become the youngest person to circumnavigate the globe in a sailboat, solo, nonstop, and unassisted. At 16 years old, her determination and spirit exemplified the sentiment, "The only easy day was yesterday."

Before setting sail on her journey, Jessica faced significant mental and physical challenges. She needed to prepare herself for the daunting task ahead. This involved extensive training, learning about the intricacies of her boat, understanding global weather patterns, and preparing for emergencies. The media and some in the sailing community were vocal in doubting her capability because of her age and inexperience.

On October 18, 2009, Jessica began her journey. Throughout her voyage, which lasted more than 200 days, she faced numerous challenges that tested her resolve. Every day was a battle as she withstood violent weather, a capsized boat, and the sheer loneliness of sailing alone at sea for months.

On May 15, 2010, after 210 days at sea, Jessica Watson sailed into Sydney Harbor, achieving her dream. Not only had she sailed around the world solo at such a young age, but she had also overcome challenges that would've daunted even the most experienced sailors. Each day had its difficulties, and with every sunrise, she prepared herself for them.

Jessica's journey is a testament to unyielding resilience and determination. No matter who you are or what you've achieved, you must admit that traveling around the globe in a one-person sailboat at 16 is more than just an accomplishment. It's an incredible example of achieving success through tenacity and grit.

Her story should prompt us to ask: if she could harness her inner strength in such a remarkable way, what steps can I take to foster grit in my life?

Retired commander of U.S. Special Operations Command and decorated Navy SEAL officer, Admiral William H. McRaven addresses the significance of the mantra "The only easy day was yesterday" in his book *The Wisdom of the Bullfrog*:

> But it doesn't mean that every day has to exhaust you. Being a great leader doesn't mean you have to have superhuman strength. It only means that you have to recognize that it will require effort, every day. And some days you just won't bring it. That's okay. That's normal. But then, bring it the next day, or the next. You will only fail as a leader when you think today is going to be easier than yesterday.[3]

24

The Game-Changing Power of Diversity

The value of a diverse team is its capacity to challenge the norm or group think and thus boost organizational performance and improve decision-making.
—Yrthya Dinzey-Flores

FOOTBALL HAS ALWAYS been more than just a game to me; it's been a guide, teaching me lessons about life and how the world works. One of the greatest lessons it's taught me, which often surprises people, is the value of embracing diversity. Although I didn't fully grasp this until college, it has since become a guiding principle.

Let's step back to understand why this was such a revelation. My childhood was, by all accounts, a comfortable one. My parents, who've always been my rock, provided my brother and me with a loving, stable home. We were fortunate to never worry about the essentials, like food and shelter, and could even indulge in sports, hobbies, and vacations. The adversity and challenges I encountered in my teenage years were self-induced.

Life shifted gears, though, when I transitioned from high school sports to college athletics. Until then, my teammates were friends I'd known for years, with similar upbringings and life experiences. In college, that familiarity vanished. Suddenly, my teammates were strangers from different walks of life, each with stories and struggles.

For example, some had childhoods defined by not knowing where their next meal would come from, and others didn't have the support of both parents like I did.

This shift was an eye-opener. Immersing myself among teammates with varied and rich backgrounds quietly reshaped my worldview. Now, looking back, I can see what a gift that was. In navigating these diverse team dynamics, I learned the importance of connecting with, learning from, and valuing people whose life experiences and viewpoints differ significantly from yours.

Despite the advancements we've made as a society, there's still a tendency for organizations and leaders to stick with what's familiar, often hiring employees and forming teams based on shared values and perspectives. It's a safety net of sorts, but one that stifles growth and innovation. This lesson from the gridiron extends far beyond the game, pushing us to harness the benefits of diversity in daily life.

Shattering the Conventional

Although this will not surprise you, I'll say it anyway: I'm not a diversity expert. So, when I discuss diversity and the pivotal role leaders play in it, it's not through the lens of a traditional diversity, equity, and inclusion (DE&I) approach. Instead, it's about fostering a team's trajectory toward victory and enhanced performance through a genuine blend of varied perspectives and skill sets. Embracing diversity is not about bowing down to social pressure, meeting compliance standards, or satisfying stakeholders; instead, it's about understanding diversity as an essential driver of success, growth, and innovation.

Too often, many organizations fall into superficial advocacy, portraying an image of diversity and inclusion that, on closer scrutiny, reveals nothing more than an ill-advised public relations strategy. It's a surface-level approach to doing what seems right without rooting those actions in authentic, transformative change.

Leaders who spearhead transformative journeys understand that diversifying a team extends well beyond the moral or ethical implications and into the practical. They recognize the substantial value of a melting pot of perspectives, skills, and experiences. Football has always showcased this powerful truth through talented individuals from various backgrounds combining their strengths to achieve a collective goal.

Such unity can only happen when leaders dare to dismantle the old, comfortable narratives. It demands we step away from familiar, established norms and seek strength in a broader cross-section of individuals. It's about recognizing and valuing a simple truth: diversity in talent, experience, and background fuels the collective engine of team success.

Building a diverse, inclusive, and high-performing team necessitates a transformative approach to recruitment, challenging the traditional methods organizations use to attract talent. Many of these frameworks have long existed, but are they yielding the desired results?

During my three years working with a hospitality organization, I observed a pattern in their approach to talent acquisition that prevented them from achieving their goal. In monthly and quarterly meetings, there was a persistent focus on recruiting talent to comply with diversity standards, often initiated by leaders expressing frustration at the scarcity of highly skilled candidates. However, after briefly discussing the problem, they'd shift to their existing recruitment strategy, which they'd unanimously agree was acceptable.

This scenario revealed a critical gap in perception. The top leaders at these meetings would repeatedly deploy HR to college career fairs and rely on word-of-mouth recommendations for suitable leads. Then, be surprised when the talent pool wasn't diverse. This approach overlooks a fundamental truth: searching for talent in the same place, using the same methods, will inevitably lead to the same outcomes.

A breakthrough occurred after one of our all-day meetings. The organization didn't overhaul its plan but acknowledged the need for change. This shift in mindset was crucial. For leaders to build diverse and dynamic teams, they must innovate and expand recruitment practices beyond the comfort of traditional methods. Here's the three-step process the organization outlined to diversify its recruitment strategy:

1. Highlight the skills and competencies required for each vacant position instead of relying on generic job descriptions based on qualifications and experience.

2. Identify three industries, other than its own, where it believes the talent possesses skill sets that could be advantageous and transferable.

3. Senior leaders pledged to actively participate in the recruitment process instead of delegating it to HR.

Once the organization shifted its strategy based on these three steps the following year, it succeeded in gradually filling pivotal positions and made significant strides in improving diversity metrics. The leadership team succeeded by consciously seeking talent in untapped areas, prioritizing skills over traditional qualifications, and ensuring they took ownership of the initiative.

It's important to acknowledge that building a diverse, high-performing team is a gradual process that doesn't materialize overnight. But a great starting point is reevaluating our approaches to recruiting top talent; such steps are essential in steering us toward a more inclusive and dynamic future.

The Quintessential Edge of Diversity

The primary advantage of purposefully embracing and leveraging team diversity is its capacity to unlock and amplify collective intelligence, the basis of innovative problem-solving and strategic thinking. While diverse thought strengthens and nurtures collective intelligence, its impact stretches beyond theoretical assumptions, embedding itself in real-world applications and demonstrable outcomes.

Research has shown that complex problem-solving capability is not merely a derivative of individual intelligence or expertise within a team. A study highlighted that teams with a diverse composition, embodying varied experiences, nationalities, and backgrounds, tend to outperform homogenous teams.[1]

This is especially true when it comes to innovative problem-solving. The Boston Consulting Group conducted a global study and discovered that diverse teams are 1.7 times more likely to be market segment innovation leaders and generate 19% more revenue. This study found a link between diversity in management positions and company-wide innovation, supporting the argument that diverse teams perform better and generate more profits.[2]

Let's explore this concept through the story of Margaret Hamilton, a computer scientist who coined the term *software engineer* in the early 1960s to describe her work to friends and family.[3] While leading the software engineering division at the MIT Instrumentation Laboratory, the National Aeronautics and Space Administration (NASA) tapped Hamilton to develop the onboard flight software for the *Apollo* space program. Hamilton didn't have a background in aeronautics; she came from a different field, bringing a fresh, unique perspective to the project team.

This divergent thinking allowed her to identify and mitigate an issue many other team members overlooked. An issue that, if left undetected, would've resulted in a critical mission failure during the 1969 moon landing. Hamilton's unique skill set, which differed from her aeronautics-focused colleagues, proved instrumental in the United States winning the space race against its cold-war adversaries, forever shaping world history.

In the same way, teams that bring together people from different backgrounds gain access to a wide range of viewpoints and insights, which helps them solve complex problems using refined and multifaceted methods. In an increasingly interconnected and interdependent time, the power of diversity cannot simply be an afterthought. Its integration within the fabric of an organization enhances collective intelligence and ensures a resilient, adaptive, and innovative progression through the challenges and opportunities ahead.

The potency of different perspectives and experiences contributes to a holistic approach to problem-solving and decision-making, embodying the undeniable strength of genuine diversity.

The Path Forward

Understanding and implementing are worlds apart because intention can never outweigh action, no matter how noble. So, how do we, as leaders, acknowledge and integrate diversity in our teams and organizations? It comes down to a few crucial actions:

1. **Expand Your Talent Search:** Identifying and recruiting exceptional talent requires venturing beyond familiar territories. We must dismantle rigid protocols, broaden our scouting horizons,

and leave behind outdated methodologies. Proactive leaders must curate a strategic list, identifying unconventional avenues to explore talent. A hallmark of a transformational leader is recognizing potential in unexpected places and having the drive to pursue it.

2. **Continuously Mitigate Bias:** Actively seek individuals whose journeys diverge from your own, embracing those from other cultures and environments. A leader's ability to consciously sidestep personal biases and welcome individuals different from themselves catalyzes transformative power within a team.

3. **Champion Collective Power:** Actively enlist insight from all corners of your organization, especially when facing nuanced challenges or pivotal decisions. Leverage the abundant and varied perspectives within your team, even those traditionally outside decision-making circles. Diverse input, centered on a unified mission, anchors the team in a solid foundation of multidimensional viewpoints.

4. **Infuse Diverse Strategies:** While assembling a diverse team is a great start, a heterogeneous approach to operational strategies must complement it. In practice, this means revitalizing meeting structures, escaping functional monotony, and experimenting with innovative approaches. The goal is to ensure the multifaceted nature of your team is mirrored in your methodologies, thereby amplifying the team's impact and efficacy.

5. **Foster an Inclusive Culture:** Cultivating a culture that welcomes and champions diversity is paramount—one where voices are heard, valued, and respected. Develop platforms and forums where team members can share their thoughts, experiences, and insights. Implement mentorship and development programs that ensure every team member can grow and thrive. Emphasize the importance of mutual respect, understanding, and learning, fostering an environment where everyone, regardless of their background, feels seen, heard, and integral to the team's success.

6. **Become Talent-Driven:** The fundamental idea behind talent-driven organizations is that talent drives strategy rather than

strategy-defining talent. A trait of organizations that prioritizes talent is a focus on identifying, cultivating, and optimizing this asset. It all begins with leaders assuming the role of primary talent recruiters.[4]

Piecing Together the Diversity Puzzle

A diverse culture doesn't just happen; it's a strategic puzzle that requires more than token gestures and superficial compliance. It takes effort to build a diverse team, which means doing things a little differently than we're used to. Still, I'm not saying compromise your exacting standards or hire less qualified candidates in the name of diversity—again, this is not about DE&I. Instead, rethink and reshape your recruiting process to ensure it is inclusive, expansive, and perpetually aligned with an undeniably diverse future. Seek the brightest, most qualified individuals for each role; just be prepared to follow that path wherever it may lead.

Change is difficult and demands a steadfast commitment to expanding your outlook, celebrating collective intellect, and refreshing your operational strategies to reflect modern team dynamics. This is not a call to celebrate diversity but to actively support it. We can navigate complex challenges and lead our teams to success by embracing different perspectives, backgrounds, and experiences.

PART

VII

The Greater Good > Isolated Greatness

25

Purposeful Leadership: Making a Difference Beyond Personal Achievement

People don't buy what you do. They buy why you do it.

—Simon Sinek

HAVE YOU EVER listened to an accountant describe their job in detail? Even if you possess a basic understanding of the field, you're unlikely to say it's inspiring, meaningful work. That didn't stop accounting firm KPMG from setting out to convince employees that its work could change the world. The company already held a significant market share, and its engagement and morale were strong, but it wanted to reach for greatness. KPMG developed a strategic plan, invested resources, and introduced an initiative focused on reframing accounting from a job defined by crunching numbers to a career built on a deeper purpose.

The industry leader aimed to inspire its employees, which required a message everyone could rally around. Leadership understood that messaging was vital; they began developing a powerful message that employees could feel. After extensive research, countless interviews, and hours of group testing, KPMG had its purpose statement: *Inspire Confidence. Empower Change.*

While powerful, the company knew that in-depth research and a clever slogan were useless without integrating it into the core of what it does. Focused on evoking an emotional connection, the company released a video celebrating the impact of employees on their clients, communities, and society; it encouraged them to think of themselves as professionals who help families make sound financial choices rather than simply as auditors. The video was more than a feel-good project and chronicled the firm's role in historical events, such as certifying Nelson Mandela's victory in South Africa's 1994 presidential election. It ended with a crucial question: "What do we do here at KPMG?"

The response from employees was resounding: "We Shape History!" The company rode this momentum by challenging employees to reflect on how their work makes a difference. Leadership set a goal of 10,000 stories; they received 42,000. They were astounded by the results. Less than a year into the initiative, 85% of workers agreed that KPMG was a great place to work, and in the following year, that number increased to 89%. More than 60% of employees reported feeling prouder of their work than before the initiative. When *Fortune* magazine's annual 100 Best Places to Work hit newsstands, KPMG topped the list—a record among the Big Four accounting firms. This groundswell also impacted the firm's financial performance, which allowed it to rise to the ranks of the Big Four in terms of growth.[1]

What lesson can we take from KPMG? The firm demonstrated that there's extraordinary power in leading with purpose. This is not some passing trend; it's a transformative force that can catalyze lasting change. Decide what you stand for as an organization, team member, or individual, and let the world know.

Effect and Impact

At first, developing an inspiring purpose may sound great, but is it worth putting aside your other responsibilities? If there's a desire to attract and retain top talent, boost performance, and improve team morale, then the answer is an unequivocal "yes." Exploring the concept of purpose in business is not about toeing the line of corporate social responsibility (CSR)—far from it. While today's CSR is little more than a public relations strategy used to manipulate public opinion and increase profits, true purpose is the core of an organization's existence.

Let's look at an example to understand the importance of aligning purpose with action. While serving as CEO of PepsiCo, Indra Nooyi identified a rising trend—the market's pivot toward healthier choices.[2] However, her response was more than an attempt to boost sales; Nooyi recognized an opportunity to galvanize her workforce and invest in the future by aligning the company's objectives with the broader cultural shift. This wasn't about chasing market trends but forging a connection with employees that echoed changing societal values.

During an interview with Adi Ignatius, editor and chief of *Harvard Business Review*, Indra Nooyi said, "Purpose is not about giving money away for social responsibility. It's about fundamentally changing how to make money . . . to deliver performance—to help ensure that PepsiCo is a . . . company where young people want to work."

Nooyi's vision was twofold: it addressed the evolving consumer preferences for healthier products and created a narrative that employees could rally behind. This narrative told of a company contributing to societal well-being, a cause more significant than chasing profits. By integrating this purpose-driven strategy, Nooyi led a transformation within PepsiCo that positioned the company as a forerunner in addressing market trends and employee motivation. Through this, we observe the potency of aligning a firm's strategic endeavors with meaningful purpose, creating a symbiotic relationship between market responsiveness and employee engagement.[3]

Why should other companies invest in discovering their purpose rather than simply turning to optic-driven CSR? Well, compelling data shows its power.

A study conducted by LinkedIn reveals that 71% of professionals would take a pay cut to work for an organization that shares their values.[4] Similarly, research from Deloitte found that 80% of Millennials who planned on staying with their current employer for at least five years believe the company has a strong sense of purpose.[5] Furthermore, the EY Beacon Institute and *Harvard Business Review* analytic services report revealed that 89% of executives believe a strong sense of collective purpose drives employee satisfaction, and 84% say it can affect an organization's ability to transform.[6]

These numbers speak volumes and reflect a reality where *leading with purpose* is not a slogan direct from Madison Avenue but a catalytic force driving performance, retention, and achievement. These are not just statistics but a call to build something meaningful. Purpose is a compass that guides us and an unseen force that galvanizes, unites, and propels us forward. It's about rising above the transactional to recognize that it's not what you take that matters but rather what you leave behind.

Are you still unconvinced and considering waiting for this to run its course?

Let me stop you right there because society's expectations surrounding professional purpose are only growing. A 2012 Net Impact report titled *Job Security and Meaningful Work in High Demand for Today's Workforce* found that 65% of workers said that finding a job that allows them to contribute to society is important to them. In the same report, Net Impact CEO Liz Maw explained, "Employees today don't want to check their values at the door when they arrive at their jobs, and the ability to live and work with strong social meaning is clearly important." She says, "Young people in college . . . see making a social impact as a critical part of their career . . . these resilient and optimistic students are leading with their values."[7]

That was in 2012; how have things changed since? A 2022 Ernst & Young white paper shows that 84% of employees believe it's "very important" that their company has a purpose that contributes to society.[8] Research conducted by McKinsey & Company in 2022 revealed that 70% of employees say when their work has a purpose and meaning, their performance increases, and they are half as likely to look for a new job.[9]

The Baseline: Discovering Team Purpose

Ready to make a greater impact as a leader? First, we must ensure our organization has a solid, meaningful purpose; if it doesn't, we must create one using the company's ethos and mission. This is more than a superficial exercise of stringing together inspirational phrases or resorting to clichéd expressions in the hopes of stumbling on something that resonates. Purposeful leadership is built on aligning the unglamorous yet indispensable work you and your team do day after day with a purpose more meaningful than making money. Instilling the pursuit of purpose in daily operations helps cultivate a culture that values authentic connection and legacy over temporary victories.

Incorporating the framework from Hubert Joly's book, *The Heart of Business*, can significantly delineate and fortify an organizational purpose. He poses a series of questions that serve as a lens to evaluate intrinsic strength and fuel an introspective journey that transcends the superficial. Joly defines purpose as an intersection of these four questions:

- What human needs are you attempting to address?
- What are you uniquely good at?
- What are you passionate about?
- How are you going to make money?[10]

Diving into Joly's questions can illuminate the core of your organization. When you think about human needs, you identify the vacuum your organization intends to fill in people's lives. Meanwhile, pinpointing what you are uniquely skilled at helps distinguish your organization in a crowded and ultra-competitive environment. But it doesn't end there. Reflecting on what ignites passion among your team can fuel the drive needed to push through challenges. Last, considering how you'll sustain yourself financially is a grounding factor, ensuring your purpose is paired with a viable business model.

In bringing these questions to the discussion table, you're not just crafting a purpose statement; you're initiating a thought-provoking dialogue that can lead to understanding your organizational ethos. This process helps blend aspirations and practicality, which nurtures a culture of purpose-driven excellence and long-term sustainability.

Leading with Purpose

Harnessing a deeper understanding of the transformative power of a purpose-driven organizational shift, it begs the question: how can leaders seamlessly embed this purpose into their day? Discussing purpose while contradicting it with our actions is a recipe for stagnation.

As my friend and best-selling author Jon Gordon says, a company can have the best mission statement, but its impact will be minimal if its employees aren't on a mission themselves.

The same is true for evolving into a more purpose-driven team; a leader's actions matter exponentially more than any initiative, survey, or inspirational mantra. The best way to ensure team members are purpose-driven is for leaders to set the standard. The magnitude of influence a purpose-driven leader wields is immeasurable; a single ripple they create can become a tidal wave, influencing countless people in its wake.

While many organizations wear their mission statements and values like a badge of honor, the real challenge is that not all leaders do. Cultivating this intrinsic connection is pivotal as an ever-present compass that steers us toward purposeful leadership. Developing such a connection strengthens the capacity to lead by serving as a reminder to keep purpose front and center. I advocate that all leaders create a personalized mission statement infused with their core values. Give it a try; you'll be amazed by the results.

Create Your Leadership Mission Statement

Using a notebook and pen, use this as an outline for creating your leadership mission statement. When approached with a growth mindset and an open perspective, this becomes an invaluable guide to transformative leadership.

STEP 1: *Reflect on Your Core Values and Beliefs*   Begin this introspective journey by connecting with your fundamental beliefs. Reflect on these prompts:

- What kind of leader do I aspire to be?
- What impact do I hope to have, personally and professionally?
- What are non-negotiables to me?

STEP 2: *Identify and Articulate Your Gifts*   Assess your gifts—the attributes that make you unique and special. Reflect on these prompts:

- How do these gifts align with my values and envisioned objectives?
- How can I bring these attributes to life more frequently?

STEP 3: *Define Your Leadership Aspirations*   Channel your aspirations into tangible goals. Reflect on these prompts:

- What are my short- and long-term goals?

- What specific actions and behaviors must I engage in to achieve them?
- What kind of legacy do I hope to leave?

STEP 4: *Crafting Your Leadership Mission Statement*   Craft your leadership mission statement using the insights garnered from this exercise. As you do, try to keep in mind the following:

- Your leadership statement should be clear and concise.
- Your leadership statement should reflect your values, goals, and character.
- Avoid overthinking it. The utmost priority, whether a sentence, multiple sentences, or a paragraph, is to accurately convey your identity, aspirations, and the impact you aim to have as a leader.

Endless Possibilities

We all want our lives to be about more than punching the clock. The good news is that no matter who you are or what you're facing, you control the level of purpose you approach the day with. The potential for affecting radical change and making a lasting difference in the world is virtually limitless. To have such far-reaching influence, leaders must do more than set objectives; they must steer their teams in a focused direction with purpose leading the way.

In his best-selling book *Start with Why*, Simon Sinek brilliantly captures this frame of mind:

Imagine if every organization started with WHY. Decisions would be simpler. Loyalties would be greater. Trust would be a common currency. If our leaders were diligent about starting with WHY, optimism would reign and innovation would thrive. No matter the size of the organization, no matter the industry, no matter the product or the service, if we all take some responsibility to start with WHY and inspire others to do the same, then, together, we can change the world.[11]

The takeaway: When you let your "WHY" dictate your PURPOSE, the possibilities are endless.

26

The True Price of Transformational Leadership

Leaders sacrifice themselves for the good of others.

—Patrick Lencioni

THE COST OF transformational and outstanding leadership is sacrifice, as selfless service differentiates great leaders from everyone else. Nothing of value comes easy; we must remember this and apply it to all aspects of life. While improving our performance is great, bringing out the best in others and forming a high-performing team is even better. But how can we scale the commitments, standards, and impact of stellar leadership?

When asked to imagine a transformational leader, most people picture someone influential and charismatic. That's because people automatically associate leadership with superiority and prestige. Those who've earned the reputation of being exceptional leaders are shaking their heads right now; what do they know that we don't? They know that impact-driven leadership isn't defined by accolades and praise but by service and sacrifice. These are the cornerstones of transformational leadership, yet they are topics rarely discussed and responsibilities infrequently accepted.

The concept of sacrifice is akin to eating a diet of healthy foods. We know it's good for us and has potential benefits, but we often give in to the temptation of the less healthy option. At that moment, we do not consider how our choices will affect us 5, 10, or even 20 years later. That's because what we want more than anything is that momentary comfort, which is why we choose the cheeseburger over the salad. The concept of making sacrifices that maximize and cascade the impact of leadership follows a similar pattern. It's too easy to take shortcuts and convince ourselves that what we do today won't matter down the line, but it will.

The cold, hard truth is that this doesn't become less of a problem the more success we attain. Quite the opposite; the more success and admiration we receive, the more likely we will become deceptively complacent. Whether we're in a cubicle at the start of our career or the corner office at the height of it, we must focus on acquiring the mindsets and skills needed to prioritize long-term excellence over immediate comfort. Our willingness to sacrifice these comforts significantly impacts what we will and will not achieve.

Since you're choosing the road to transformational leadership, it's only fitting that you know the truth: leadership = sacrifice. Those who want to make a lasting impact—leaders like you and me—must prepare to make five significant sacrifices (Figure 26.1). While these sacrifices are ongoing, the transformational leader recognizes that they are but a small price to pay for the impact they facilitate.

The Five Sacrifices of Transformational Leadership:

1. Weight of Responsibility.
2. Invisible Investment.
3. Individual versus Collective.

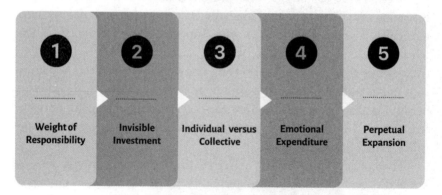

Figure 26.1   Five Sacrifices of Transformational Leadership.

4. Emotional Expenditure.
5. Perpetual Expansion.

1. Weight of Responsibility: Navigating the Delicate Balance

Decision-making carries a significantly heavier burden for those in leadership positions or who aspire to be in the future. Making choices that impact us is difficult enough, but making decisions that affect the livelihood of those who rely on us is exponentially more complicated. Leaders learn early on that looking out for the people under their charge often requires putting personal preferences, convenience, and self-interests on the back burner. Wearing the mantle of leadership requires an infusion of selfless drive, unwavering dedication, and personal accountability. Investigating the weight of responsibility provides a broader perspective on the cost of leadership.

- **Decision Complexity:** The decisions leaders must make daily are rarely binary. They cover a wide range of possibilities, each with its drawbacks and advantages. The critical thinking and foresight required to make such decisions are much higher than those required to make ordinary ones. Each decision requires a delicate balance of many factors, including those of various stakeholders.
- **Ripple Effect:** Like the way a stone thrown into a pond causes a chain reaction, so do our choices. One strategic decision may affect an entire industry, while another may lead to an organizational shift impacting team or market dynamics. Recognizing and accounting for these ripples before throwing the rock demonstrates the multifaceted nature of a leader's role.
- **Embracing Empathy:** Critique or second-guessing is inevitable when making significant decisions. There are times of uncertainty for all leaders, no matter how much experience they have. As a leader, you must accept that you will never be able to please everyone. A leader's actions will inevitably be met with mixed reactions. While it's impossible to please everyone, we can harness the efficacy of empathy by considering how our choices, moves, and bets affect others.

- **Prioritizing the "We" Factor:** The endless balance between segmented objectives and those of the larger organization and team is a defining aspect of the weight of responsibility. Transformational leaders know they must sacrifice the personal for the good of the collective. These actions are more than selfless service; they demonstrate a leader's commitment to the overarching mission. This sacrifice often ensnares those pursuing leadership for the wrong reasons, but authentic leaders are unaffected because they always have the team's best interests at heart.

The weight of responsibility is a complex test that demands a strategic approach, emotional maturity, moral rectitude, and a firm resolve to do what's right for the greater good. Transformational leaders take an in-depth account of the situation and make decisions that allow them to successfully navigate their complex web of responsibilities.

2. Invisible Investment: Beyond the Ticking Clock

Transformational leaders are aware that their time is finite. Whether it's an unforeseen crisis, a troubled team member, or a last-minute project review, leaders often must put their plans on hold. Accepting fewer days off, more late nights, and missing family dinners is a sacrifice of time for the greater good. Arguably, time is a leader's most valued commodity. It's more than just a countdown of hours, minutes, and seconds; it represents their dedication, adaptability, and devotion to the mission. Understanding leaders' complex relationship with time helps shed light on the difficulties and challenges.

- **Always-On Paradigm:** We live in a hyper-connected world, and ease of access results in a leader's professional obligations extending outside the office. The expectation of being "always on" to make crucial decisions, manage teams across time zones, and handle unexpected events further blurs the lines between work and leisure time.
- **Juggling Multiple Timelines:** Leaders don't just exist in the here and now; they also think about past lessons, present problems, and future possibilities. This calls for a level of mental flexibility that's taxing. Learning from yesterday's mistakes, dealing

with today's pressing issues, and planning for several potential futures is an ongoing process that extends far beyond the typical workday.

- **Emotional Time Tax:** Besides the obvious monetary cost, leaders must also factor in the intangible cost of their time. Thinking about past choices, stressing over colleagues, and planning takes mental energy. Many leaders find themselves thinking through situations to gain perspective during their free time, which, for many, comes as they lie awake at night. If this happening day after day, week after week, and year after year isn't emotionally taxing, I don't know what is.

Time is a multidimensional concept with unseen implications, especially for leaders. Those committed to making a lasting impact give far more than time; they're also emotionally, mentally, and physically invested in ensuring a successful outcome for all involved. Leadership is a testament to tenacity, commitment, and the never-ending quest for improvement.

3. Individual Versus Collective: The Art of Group-Centric Leadership

Leaders must always focus on the bigger picture while ensuring their vision and plans meet their team's current needs. This means often sacrificing personal ambitions and projects; these daily sacrifices are best thought of as always putting the group first. The path to extraordinary leadership is rarely linear, as leaders must often navigate their ambitions around those of the group, a dynamic that defines transformational leadership. Let's take a closer look at the complexities of this balance.

- **Art of Compromise:** Despite its unfavorable reputation in today's politically charged climate, compromise remains an essential tool in the leader's arsenal. It's about finding a happy medium where personal desire coexists with and complements organizational needs. The ability to compromise effectively calls for wisdom, adaptability, and an expansive perspective.

- **Emotional Quotient (EQ):** It's not just a strategic move to prioritize the organization's needs over your wants and desires. The emotional repercussions of abandoning a beloved project or putting off a personal ambition are a common source of stress. Leaders with a high EQ can better deal with their emotions without slowing the decision-making process.
- **Long-Term Vision and Short-Term Desires:** While organizational needs tend to align with long-term objectives, the needs of individuals often come from a place of emotion. Leaders can weigh the benefits of immediate gratification against the longer-term effects of choices that strengthen development and continuity. In doing so, they ensure the organization's continued success and often exceed expectations in unexpected ways.

When weighing individual ambitions against collective benefit, it's not a matter of picking one but finding common ground to advance both. This exemplifies the complexity and nuance of authentic leadership, as it requires selflessness and flexibility.

4. Emotional Expenditure: The Hidden Strains of Leading

Like everyone else, leaders have emotional limits; they're only human. Still, we expect leaders to be a source of strength and optimism during adversity—a rock, even when everyone around them is crumbling. This may involve masking their emotions, concerns, or fears to instill confidence in others. While the emotional dimension of leadership is intangible, it plays a pivotal role in the leader's well-being and that of those they lead.

- **Emotional Balancing Act:** Emotional balance is something leaders must constantly maintain. One must keep in touch with their emotions, which gives them access to vital intuition and insight. On the other hand, they must maintain a strong front, particularly during trying times, to ensure the team sees hope rather than fear.

- **Reservoir of Resilience:** Leaders must dig deep when times are tough. They become the rocks that give us footing amid the waves. Although they're not immune to doubts or fears, they've mastered the art of emotional compartmentalization— knowing when to allow themselves to feel things and when to put those feelings aside.

5. Perpetual Expansion: Journey of Continuous Growth

The public often sees leadership roles as the pinnacle of a successful career, but transformational leaders maintain a growth mindset to make a lasting difference. This perpetual expansion requires growth in perspective, competencies, and learning. Sacrificing pride is vital because achieving power is not the end goal but the beginning of a new chapter based on service. Being content is never a viable option for transformational leaders.

- **The Myth of "Having Arrived":** Assuming a leadership role and career advancement is impressive; the false sense of accomplishment that comes with it can be extremely harmful. The challenges leaders face are constantly in flux, meaning we must maintain a growth mindset and remain agile and nimble enough to shift instantly.
- **Humility to Learn:** All great leaders exhibit humility, which is the understanding that no matter how much they've accomplished, there's always more to learn. This requires putting pride aside and welcoming input from all team members, including those with less experience. There's truth in the adage that we can learn something from each person we meet; all we must do is be humble enough to recognize the lessons when they come.
- **Curating a Growth Environment:** Leaders must prepare those around them to be lifelong learners by modeling the behavior they want to have mirrored back. Leaders can keep their teams and organizations agile and competitive by encouraging new ideas, providing feedback, and investing in continuous training.

This sacrifice becomes extremely hard, especially when things are moving quickly.

Honor in Sacrifice

Why would anyone want to be a leader if they knew what was in store for them? The transformational leader doesn't make sacrifices for the sake of making sacrifices, but to make a lasting impact and bring about positive change.

The rewards of leading a team to victory, helping others become their best, and fostering a culture of development and innovation justify these sacrifices. An unbreakable bond of trust and loyalty is formed when team members observe their leader making sacrifices for the group's good.

Many people gravitate toward leadership for the wrong reasons—namely, lust for power and recognition—but the reality of sacrifice quickly weeds out the pretenders. While most people would avoid sacrifice, those destined to be transformational leaders inherently know doing so is a surefire way to leave a positive mark on the world.

Why does transformational leadership require great sacrifice? Because, in the words of President John F. Kennedy, "To whom much is given, much is required."

27

Leaving a Legacy: Leading Beyond Self

What you leave behind is not what is engraved in stone monuments, but what is woven into the lives of others.

—Pericles

ON A DARK, gloomy Thursday morning, I arrived at the headquarters of a prominent retailer a few hours ahead of a meeting with the leadership team. We had a full agenda planned, and I couldn't wait to start. As I headed toward the conference room through a maze of dark, empty hallways, I noticed a soft glow of white light and the sounds of smooth jazz coming from a distant office. My curiosity got the best of me.

As I approached the office, I saw a key member of senior leadership scribbling notes into a moleskin notebook. He had been with the company for 15 years, and everyone in the industry admired him. I gently knocked on the door, which was partially open. After saying "hello," I asked why he was there earlier than everyone else.

He lowered his reading glasses and said, "Hey, good morning, Matt. It's great to see you. I arrived early so I could have some quiet time to think."

The seriousness in his expression piqued my interest, so I probed further: "Oh, yeah? What's on your mind this morning?" He closed his notebook, using the pen to hold his place, and leaned back in his chair.

Instead of answering, he gently swayed back and forth as he carefully considered his response. After a few moments, he replied, "Matt, I've enjoyed a remarkable career and have accomplished far more than I imagined possible. I've made a lot of money doing work that I wake up in the morning excited about." He paused; it was clear that something was bothering him, so I said, "In my opinion, that's a well-lived life, and I know many people who would love to have accomplished half of what you have. So, what's wrong?"

He stopped swaying, thought momentarily, and asked, "When it's all said and done, what does all this success mean? I have a wonderful family and a fulfilling career, and I'm grateful for those things, but as I get older, a question keeps me up at night: what will I leave besides material wealth? What's my contribution to the world? What's my legacy?"

Reassessing Life's True Value

Early in our careers, even midway through, we concentrate on future success. Focusing on the present, worrying about the future, and questioning what truly matters are all part of being human. In other words, it's completely natural. As we age, the totality of our experiences begins shifting our thoughts and priorities. Our focus is no longer consumed by attaining success, worrying about what others think, or problems from the past over which we have no control. Instead, our thoughts become preoccupied with regret as we grieve missed opportunities; we wonder if there could have been more to life than money, power, and success.

Most people reach the same conclusion as life begins winding down: accomplishments and financial success mean little. Like it or not, it's something we all face eventually. Not convinced? If you have a friend or family member who had a near-death experience, respectfully ask what matters to them now that they have a second chance at life.

Hospice nurses on palliative care units can attest to my statement. For years, hospice nurse and counselor Bronnie Ware cared for terminally ill patients with a prognosis of less than 12 weeks. Ware shared that patients most regretted not spending more time with family, failing to stay in contact with friends, and not expressing their emotions more often. While each of these ranked highly, she said the most common regret was patients allowing fear and societal expectations to prevent them from pursuing their dreams and aspirations.[1]

The purpose of life and leadership is to make a meaningful impact on others. Technology executive Sheryl Sandberg explained, "Leadership is about making others better as a result of your presence and making sure that impact lasts in your absence." This isn't to downplay the importance of striving for excellence; it's simply a gentle reminder not to be so consumed by today's challenges that you forget to look at the bigger picture. Someday, we will recognize that those small things were far more significant than we could have imagined, and it will keep us up at night.

Embrace Each Day: Leading with Passion and Purpose

Connecting with a deeper purpose can significantly enhance our impact as leaders. It's all about how we approach each day, whether we're passively going through the motions or actively making a difference.

Transformational leaders are often mistaken for high achievers. While they achieve a lot, their strength lies in bringing out the best in others. This leadership style is built on passionate and purposeful engagement. You may even know a few of these leaders—they never brag and are always first to let others shine. They're ready to tackle the next challenge with renewed passion and purpose, even after hitting a significant goal. While this may seem unhealthy and unrealistic to some, many are curious about how they achieve such a consistent drive.

Research has shown that contemplating mortality can lead to a fuller, more meaningful life.[2] A study by the University of Missouri–Columbia found that thinking about death can encourage better health choices, promote positive behavioral changes, and foster deeper connections with others.[3]

Many leaders find a renewed sense of passion and purpose when they reflect on life's impermanence. It allows them to visualize their legacy, helping them work backward to their current reality and lead with more intention and clarity. This reflection can be a powerful motivator to leave a legacy and drive positive change within our teams. It's about igniting a fire within that remains lit when faced with challenges, a flame that inspires us to carve our path rather than being swayed by external factors.

Here's a practical approach that I have found beneficial and witnessed directly impact hundreds of leadership teams:

1. **Reflect on Your Legacy:** How would your loved ones, coworkers, and team members remember you if today were your last day? Write down your impact from a third-person perspective, honestly noting the good and the bad.

2. **Sit with Your Reflections:** Reflect on what you wrote by asking yourself what on the list makes you happy and what brings up feelings of regret. Are you balancing your work and personal lives in a way that aligns with your values?

3. **Envision Your Eulogy:** Return to the third-person perspective and write down how you wish to be remembered, focusing on the impact you want to have from this point forward. Take your time with this, and let it be a tool to guide your leadership journey.

This exercise can provide a fresh perspective, helping align your daily actions with the legacy you want to leave. By keeping the bigger picture in mind, you'll find a more profound sense of fulfillment and become a more impactful leader.

While contemplating your mortality seems dark, it can facilitate adopting a more selfless leadership style. Furthermore, research by *Psychology Today* reveals that facing the finite nature of our existence helps us clarify priorities and strengthen relationships; this is pivotal in nurturing shared vision, fostering meaningful engagement, and contributing to a more profound sense of fulfillment and efficacy.[4]

The Dichotomy of Perception and Perspective

As we reach the end of the book, I want to share something that has the potential to change your leadership journey significantly. It all comes down to shifting away from perception and into perspective.

Perception is the personal lens through which we all view the world; it's subjective and unique to each person. Sharing your perception is akin to explaining the color red to someone who's never seen it for themselves—it's just not going to happen. So, is there any advantage to operating in our perception? Not at all. Relying on perception often leads to conflicts and misunderstandings; it's why there's so much arguing in the world today. People spend their time on social media, at home, and in the office trying to convince others to see things as they do. This cycle is like running on a treadmill—lots of energy expended but no forward movement.

Since transformational leaders understand this, they excel at rallying others around a shared vision. They don't waste time and energy trying to convince people to see the world as they do. Instead, they step outside the confines of personal perception and enter into perspective.

Perspective is learning to see the world through other people's eyes. It's visualizing yourself living their life, and with this comes understanding their feelings, concerns, and motivations. What stressors do they wake up to each morning and go to bed with each night? It involves a deeper level of empathy beyond mere agreement or understanding. By adopting a perspective-oriented approach, you can learn to anticipate the needs and responses of your team, which, in turn, equips you to lead with more foresight and effectiveness.

This shift from perception to perspective is a game-changer; it allows the strategic benefit of entering every interaction at an informational advantage. That's because, regardless of title, power, and social status, most people remain trapped in their perception, unable to see beyond their narrow viewpoint. On the other hand, transformational leaders embrace an inclusive understanding enriched by diverse thoughts and experiences.

Yes, it's challenging initially, but it becomes second nature with practice. As it does, you'll notice a profound change in your leadership and how you interact with everyone, from your spouse and kids to your boss and coworkers.

Concluding Thoughts: Growth and Service

Great leaders never stop growing. While what you've learned in this book is far from everything you'll need, it's a solid foundation for becoming the leader you aspire to be. If you make continuous growth a central tenet of your leadership philosophy, you'll position yourself to inspire your team members, address their concerns, and lead them toward shared goals. The most important thing to remember is that leadership is a life-long process. That, in essence, is the hallmark of a transformational leader—one who sees beyond oneself, understands the complexities of the human condition, and recognizes that it's an honor to serve those they lead.

Notes

Preface

1. Jaroliya, Deepak, and Gyanchandani, Rajni. (2021, August 20). Transformational leadership style: A boost or hindrance to team performance in IT sector. *Vilakshan—XIMB Journal of Management* 19(1): 87–105. https://doi.org/10.1108/xjm-10-2020-0167
2. Karaca, Hasan. (2010). The effects of transformational leadership on employees' perceived leadership effectiveness in public organizations Federal Emergency Management Agency Case. Electronic Theses and Dissertations. 1625.
3. Wojtara-Perry, Shery. (2016). The impact of transformational leadership style on the success of global virtual teams. Walden Dissertations and Doctoral Studies. 2180.
4. Bolkan, San, and Goodboy, Alan. (2009). Transformational leadership in the classroom: Fostering student learning, student participation, and teacher credibility. *Journal of Instructional Psychology* 36: 296–306.

Chapter 1

1. George, Bill. (2008, November 19). Failed leadership caused the financial crisis. *U.S. News & World Report.* https://www.usnews.com/opinion/articles/2008/11/19/failed-leadership-caused-the-financial-crisis

2. Ivanova, Irina. (2023, March 22). Silicon Valley Bank leaders "failed badly," Fed Chair Jerome Powell says. *CBS News.* https://www.cbsnews.com/news/silicon-valley-bank-leaders-failed-badly-federal-reserve-chair-jerome-powell/

Chapter 2

1. HR leadership challenges 2022. (n.d.). DDI. https://www.ddiworld.com/blog/hr-leadership-challenges-2022
2. Leadership transitions report 2021. (n.d.). DDI. https://www.ddiworld.com/research/leadership-transitions-report
3. Toesland, Finbarr. (2022, November 10). How five brands learned from digital transformation failure. *Raconteur.* https://www.raconteur.net/digital-transformation/digital-transformation-failure
4. Appelbaum, Steven, Bhardwaj, Anuj, Goodyear, Mitchell, Gong, Ting, Balasubramanian Sudha, Aravindhan, and Wei, Phil. (2022). A study of generational conflicts in the workplace. *European Journal of Business and Management Research 7:* 7–15. 10.24018/ejbmr.2022.7.2.1311

Chapter 3

1. Stein, Alan Jr. (2022, June 3). The first time I met Kobe Bryant | The unseen hours. *YouTube.* https://www.youtube.com/watch?v=pbxnzqwjKOQ
2. Prentice, W.C.H. (2022, April 11). Understanding leadership. *Harvard Business Review.* https://hbr.org/2004/01/understanding-leadership
3. O.C. Tanner. (n.d.). Leadership—Global Culture Report. https://www.octanner.com/global-culture-report/2021-leadership
4. Garton, Eric. (2017, April 25). How to be an inspiring leader. *Harvard Business Review.* https://hbr.org/2017/04/how-to-be-an-inspiring-leader
5. Salas-Vallina, Andrés, Alegre, Joaquín, and López-Cabrales, Álvaro. (2020, June 19). The challenge of increasing employees' well-being and performance: How human resource management practices and engaging leadership work together toward reaching this goal. *Human Resource Management 60(3):* 333–347. https://doi.org/10.1002/hrm.22021
6. Folkman, Joseph. (2018, November 20). The shocking statistics behind uninspiring leaders. *Forbes.* https://www.forbes.com/sites/joefolkman/2018/11/20/the-shocking-statistics-behind-uninspiring-leaders/?sh=2287f50e2b65
7. O.C. Tanner. (n.d.). Leadership—Global Culture Report. https://www.octanner.com/global-culture-report/2021-leadership

8. Is morality essential to leadership? (2017, August 23). *icma.org.* https:// icma.org/blog-posts/morality-essential-leadership
9. Bazerman, Max H. (2020, August 18). A new model for ethical leadership. *Harvard Business Review.* https://hbr.org/2020/09/a-new-model-for-ethical-leadership
10. What is leadership vision? (n.d.). *OpenGrowth.* https://www.opengrowth .com/resources/what-is-leadership-vision

Chapter 4

1. 26th Annual Global CEO Survey. (n.d.). PwC. https://www.pwc.com/ gx/en/issues/c-suite-insights/ceo-survey-2023.html
2. Machiavelli, Niccolò. (2010). *The prince: The original classic.* John Wiley & Sons.
3. Process philosophy. (2022, May 26). *Stanford Encyclopedia of Philosophy.* https://plato.stanford.edu/entries/process-philosophy/
4. Baker, Colin. (2022, September 7). What is situational leadership, and how do you practice it? Leaders.com. https://leaders.com/articles/ leadership/situational-leadership/
5. Goleman, Daniel. (2023, August 10). What makes a leader? *Harvard Business Review.* https://hbr.org/2004/01/what-makes-a-leader
6. De Smet, Aaron, Gast, Arne, Lavoie, Johanne, and Lurie, Michael. (2023, May 4). New leadership for a new era of thriving organizations. McKinsey & Company. https://www.mckinsey.com/capabilities/people-and-organizational-performance/our-insights/new-leadership-for-a-new-era-of-thriving-organizations
7. Flynn, Bill. (2021, February 27). How Alan Mulally saved Ford Motor Company with four simple decisions. Catalyst Growth Advisors. https:// catalystgrowthadvisors.com/2018/03/06/how-alan-mulally-saved-ford-motor-company-with-four-simple-decisions/

Chapter 5

1. O'Connell, Caitlin. (2020, February 4). 15 ordinary people who changed history. *Reader's Digest.* https://www.rd.com/list/inspiring-stories-15-ordinary-people-who-changed-history/
2. "Saint of 9/11" and "Hero of Flight 93": They lived very different lives but share a legacy in death. *NBC News.* https://www.nbcnews.com/ nbc-out/out-news/saint-911-hero-flight-93-lived-different-lives-share-legacy-death-rcna1979

3. Principal gave bullied kids a way to wash clothes at school, now Ellen gave him $50K. (2018, September 14). *NJ.com.* https://www.nj.com/essex/2018/09/from_newark_to_cali_west_side_hs_principal_is_a_hi.html

Chapter 6

1. Gordon, Jonathan. (2015, February 1). The dawn of marketing's new golden age. McKinsey & Company. https://www.mckinsey.com/capabilities/growth-marketingand-sales/our-insights/the-dawn-of-marketings-new-golden-age
2. Mayberry, Matt. (2023, May 30). You don't need to be "the boss" to be a leader. *Harvard Business Review.* https://hbr.org/2023/02/you-dont-need-to-be-the-boss-to-be-a-leader
3. The coaches' journal. (2022, August 7). *Twitter.* https://twitter.com/TheCoachJournal/status/1556426074929643522

Chapter 7

1. Carter, Shawn M. (2018, February 6). Here's why a $560-million powerball winner doesn't want anyone to know her name. *CNBC.* https://www.cnbc.com/2018/02/06/why-the-560-million-powerball-winner-wants-to-stay-unknown.html
2. Evans, Barry. (2023, October 2). Perpetual motion machines. *North Coast Journal.* https://www.northcoastjournal.com/humboldt/perpetual-motion-machines/Content?oid=8041450
3. Perpetual motion. Definition & Facts. (1998, July 20). *Encyclopedia Britannica.* https://www.britannica.com/science/perpetual-motion
4. Ericsson, K. Anders. (2014, August 1). The making of an expert. *Harvard Business Review.* https://hbr.org/2007/07/the-making-of-an-expert
5. What we can learn from female chess prodigies. (2022, February 25). *BBC Worklife.* https://www.bbc.com/worklife/article/20180822-what-we-can-learn-from-female-chess-prodigies
6. Judit Polgár—FIDE Commission for Women's Chess. (n.d.). http://wom.fide.com/judit-polgar/

Chapter 8

1. New study: You have 6,200 thoughts a day . . . Don't make yours negative. (2023, April 6). *NeuroGym Blog.* https://blog.myneurogym.com/new-study-you-have-6900-thoughts-a-day-dont-make-yours-negative/

2. Ng, Boon Chong. (2018, January 26). The neuroscience of growth mindset and intrinsic motivation. *Brain Sciences*. Multidisciplinary Digital Publishing Institute. https://doi.org/10.3390/brainsci8020020

3. Lake, Christopher. (2023, August 18). The Napoleon Hill Foundation. *Napoleon Hill Foundation*. https://www.naphill.org/

4. Globokar, Lidija. (2020, March 5). The power of visualization and how to use it. *Forbes*. https://www.forbes.com/sites/lidijaglobokar/2020/03/05/the-power-of-visualization-and-how-to-use-it/

5. Davis, Scott. (2018, July 29). LeBron James reportedly spends $1.5 million per year to take care of his body—Here's where it goes. *Business Insider*. https://www.businessinsider.com/how-lebron-james-spends-money-body-care-2018-7

Chapter 9

1. A theoretical understanding of transformational leadership. (n.d.). International Journal of Development Research (IJDR). https://www.journalijdr.com/theoretical-understanding-transformational-leadership

2. Duckworth, Angela. (2016). *Grit*. Simon and Schuster.

Chapter 10

1. Koch, Richard. (1999). *The 80/20 principle, expanded and updated*. Currency.

2. CliftonStrengths Online Talent Assessment. (2023, October 4). en gallop. Gallup.com. https://www.gallup.com/cliftonstrengths/en/252137/home.aspx

3. Talent Optimization Leader. (2023, September 25). The Predictive Index. https://www.predictiveindex.com/

4. Personality tests that predict performance. (2023, August 3). Hogan Assessments. https://www.hoganassessments.com/

5. Official Myers Briggs Test & Personality Assessment. (2023). MBTIonline. https://www.mbtionline.com/

6. The Nine Types. (n.d.). The Enneagram Institute. https://www.enneagraminstitute.com/

7. Keirsey Temperament Assessment. (n.d.). Keirsey Temperament Assessment. https://www.keirsey.com/

8. Strong Interest Inventory. (2023). The Myers-Briggs Company. https://www.themyersbriggs.com/en-US/Products-and-Services/Strong

9. Jeff Erlanger—Mister Rogers; Neighborhood. (2018, September 13). *Mister Rogers' Neighborhood*. https://www.misterrogers.org/articles/jeffrey-erlanger/

10. Miller, Julie. (2019, September 10). The Fred Rogers moment that made Tom Hanks bawl his eyes out. *Vanity Fair*. https://www.vanityfair.com/hollywood/2019/09/tom-hanks-mister-rogers-movie-beautiful-day-in-the-neighborhood

Chapter 11

1. NFL average TV viewership per game 2023. (2023, June 23). *Statista*. https://www.statista.com/statistics/289979/nfl-number-of-tv-viewers-usa/
2. 300 wins: Amazing stats from Bill Belichick's career. (2023, February 28). Patriots, New England. https://www.patriots.com/news/300-wins-amazing-stats-from-bill-belichick-s-career
3. Clements, Devon. (2020, January 9). What Joe Judge learned from coaching under Bill Belichick. https://www.si.com/nfl/patriots/news/what-judge-learned-from-belichick
4. Strengths based leadership: Great leaders, teams, and why people follow. (2023, August 12). Book summary. *Readingraphics*. https://readingraphics.com/book-summary-strengths-based-leadership/
5. Clifton, Jim, and Harter, Jim. (2023). *Culture shock*. Simon and Schuster.
6. Clifton, Jim, and Jim Harter. (2023). *Culture shock*. Simon and Schuster.
7. Brim, Brian J. (2023, July 21). How a focus on people's strengths increases their work engagement. *Gallup.com*. https://www.gallup.com/workplace/242096/focus-people-strengths-increases-work-engagement.aspx
8. Trapp, Roger. (2022, February 28). Why we—And those who hire us—Should focus on our Strengths. *Forbes*. https://www.forbes.com/sites/rogertrapp/2022/02/28/why-we---and-those-who-hire-us---should-focus-on-our-strengths/
9. The National Endowment for the Humanities. (n.d.). Martin Seligman and the rise of positive psychology. https://www.neh.gov/article/martin-seligman-and-rise-positive-psychology
10. Pennock, Seph Fontane. (2023, March 10). Who is Martin Seligman and what does he do? *PositivePsychology.com*. https://positivepsychology.com/who-is-martin-seligman/
11. Goud, Nelson. (2008, October). Abraham Maslow: A personal statement. *Journal of Humanistic Psychology* 48(4): 448–451. https://doi.org/10.1177/0022167808320535
12. Clifton, Jim, and Harter, Jim. (2023). *Culture shock*. Simon and Schuster.
13. The 1980 U.S. Olympic Team. (n.d.). https://www.ushockeyhalloffame.com/page/show/831562 the-1980-u-s-olympic-team

Chapter 12

1. Hubbard, Jan. (2019, March 7). It's no dream: Olympic team loses. *Los Angeles Times*. https://www.latimes.com/archives/la-xpm-1992-06-25-sp-1411-story.html
2. Writers, Staff. (2017, August 9). "We got killed": Game the Dream Team lost. *Fox Sports*. https://www.foxsports.com.au/basketball/dream-team-25-years-us-olympic-legends-killed-in-littleremembered-scrimmage-against-college-stars/news-story/87db9f49545331f6eae8974be6484688
3. Sunderland, Riley. (1964, September). Winning the hearts and minds of the people: Malaya, 1948–1960. *The Rand Corporation*. https://www.rand.org/content/dam/rand/pubs/research_memoranda/2005/RM4174.pdf
4. Holmes, Baxter. (2020, July 25). Michelin restaurants and fabulous wines: Inside the secret team dinners that have built the Spurs' dynasty. *ESPN.com*. https://www.espn.com/nba/story/_/id/26524600/secret-team-dinners-built-spurs-dynasty
5. Dewar, Carolyn, Keller, Scott, and Malhotra, Vikram (2022). *CEO excellence*. Simon and Schuster.

Chapter 13

1. *127 Hours*. IMDb. https://www.imdb.com/title/tt1542344/ (accessed January 28, 2011).
2. Barkham, Patrick. (2017, November 25). The extraordinary story behind Danny Boyle's 127 hours. *The Guardian*. https://www.theguardian.com/film/2010/dec/15/story-danny-boyles-127-hours

Chapter 15

1. Mondal, Abhijit. (2022, December 30). Super 30 selected quotes from Anne Lamott—Quotes of Quote. *Medium*. https://medium.com/quotes-of-quote/super-30-selected-quotes-from-anne-lamott-quotes-of-quote-2f920e3ac73a
2. Mental illness. (n.d.). National Institute of Mental Health. https://www.nimh.nih.gov/health/statistics/mental-illness
3. Stress in America Generation Z. (2018, October). American Psychological Association. https://www.apa.org/news/press/releases/stress/2018/stress-gen-z.pdf
4. Small, Gary W., Lee, Joo-Yeon, Kaufman, Aaron, Jalil, Jason, Siddarth, Prabha, Gaddipati, Himaja, Moody, Teena D., and Bookheimer, Susan

Y. (2020, June 30). Brain health consequences of digital technology use. Dialogues in Clinical Neuroscience. Laboratoires Servier. https://doi .org/10.31887/dcns.2020.22.2/gsmall

5. Brackett, Marc. (n.d.). Emotional intelligence. Noba. https://nobaproject .com/modules/emotional-intelligence

6. Goleman, Daniel. (2023, August 10). What makes a leader? *Harvard Business Review*. https://hbr.org/2004/01/what-makes-a-leader

7. Site-Admin. (2023, May 3). Why focus on emotional intelligence? TalentSmartEQ. https://www.talentsmarteq.com/articles/emotional-intelligence-can-boost-your-career-and-save-your-life/

8. Bradberry, Travis. (2023). *Emotional intelligence habits*. TalentSmart.

9. PRESENTING: Satya Nadella employed a "growth mindset" to overhaul Microsoft's cutthroat culture and turn it into a trillion-dollar company— Here's how he did it. (2020, March 7). *Business Insider*. https://www .businessinsider.com/microsoft-ceo-satya-nadella-company-culture-shift-growth-mindset-2020-3?op=1

10. The 10 skills you need to thrive in the fourth industrial revolution. (2023, May 31). World Economic Forum. https://www.weforum.org/ agenda/2016/01/the-10-skills-you-need-to-thrive-in-the-fourth-industrial-revolution/

Chapter 16

1. Why leaders lose their way. (2011, June 6). *HBS Working Knowledge*. https://hbswk.hbs.edu/item/why-leaders-lose-their-way

2. King, Jason. (2017, November 9). FBI bribery scandal reveals Rick Pitino wasn't just a hall of famer, but a phony. *Bleacher Report*. https:// bleacherreport.com/articles/2735653-fbi-bribery-scandal-reveals-rick-pitino-wasnt-just-a-hall-of-famer-but-a-phony

Chapter 17

1. The Herd with Colin Cowherd. (2023, September 6). Joel Klatt compares Deion Sanders to Nick Saban after Colorado win, talks LSU loss to FSU. The Herd. *YouTube*. https://www.youtube.com/ watch?v=2AFAUByFkVQ

2. How leaders inspire: Cracking the code. (2018, August 14). *Bain*. https:// www.bain.com/insights/how-leaders-inspire-cracking-the-code/

3. Schmidt, Ann. (2020, July 12). How Mary Barra led GM through its 2014 recall scandal and changed the company's culture. *Fox Business*.

https://www.foxbusiness.com/money/mary-barra-gm-2014-recall-scandal-winning-formula

4. Siddappa, Bhavya. (2022, January 5). How did Satya Nadella instill a growth mindset at Microsoft? *Medium*. https://bhavis.medium.com/how-did-satya-nadella-instill-a-growth-mindset-at-microsoft-f500fb9805c0

5. Sull, Donald. (2020, July 21). When it comes to culture, does your company walk the talk? *MIT Sloan Management Review*. https://sloanreview.mit.edu/article/when-it-comes-to-culture-does-your-company-walk-the-talk/

6. Shafi, Azher. (2023, September 5). How Elon Musk and SpaceX plan to bring humanity to Mars. *Medium*. https://medium.com/writers-blokke/how-elon-musk-and-spacex-plan-to-bring-humanity-to-mars-afd5353aee51

7. Kruse, Kevin. (2014, February 6). Why Pepsi's CEO writes to her employees' parents. *Forbes*. https://www.forbes.com/sites/kevinkruse/2014/02/06/indra-nooyi-wholehearted-leader/?sh=591d737c153e

8. Lieberman, Matthew. (2015, August 6). Should leaders focus on results, or on people? *Harvard Business Review*. https://hbr.org/2013/12/should-leaders-focus-on-results-or-on-people

9. Del Rey, Jason. (2015, November 22). Watch Jeff Bezos lay out his grand vision for Amazon's future dominance in this 1999 video. *Vox*. https://www.vox.com/2015/11/22/11620874/watch-jeff-bezos-lay-out-his-grand-vision-for-amazons-future

10. Morgan, Ronald, and Lock, Peter. (2014, March). Erin Gruwell: A biographical account of a teacher leader for change. California Association of Professors of Educational Administration. https://files.eric.ed.gov/fulltext/EJ1028874.pdf

Chapter 18

1. Friedman, Uri. (2021, August 2). How an ad campaign invented the diamond engagement ring. *The Atlantic*. https://www.theatlantic.com/international/archive/2015/02/how-an-ad-campaign-invented-the-diamond-engagement-ring/385376/

2. The cost of poor communications. (2020, July 30). SHRM. https://www.shrm.org/resourcesandtools/hr-topics/behavioral-competencies/communication/pages/the-cost-of-poor-communications.aspx

3. Communication barriers in the modern workplace. (2018). The Economist Intelligence Unit. *The Economist*. https://impact.economist.com/perspectives/sites/default/files/EIU_Lucidchart-Communication%20barriers%20in%20the%20modern%20workplace.pdf

4. Solomon, Lou. (2017, October 25). Two-thirds of managers are uncomfortable communicating with employees. *Harvard Business Review.* https://hbr.org/2016/03/two-thirds-of-managers-are-uncomfortable-communicating-with-employees

5. Decorated cave of Pont d'Arc, known as Grotte Chauvet–Pont d'Arc, Ardeche. https://whc.unesco.org/en/list/1426/ (accessed October 25, 2023).

6. Zak, Paul J. (2015, February 1). Why inspiring stories make us react: The neuroscience of narrative. PubMed Central (PMC). https://www.ncbi.nlm.nih.gov/pmc/articles/PMC4445577/

Chapter 19

1. Tremlett, Sam. (2023, February 15). Who coaches Tiger Woods? *Golf Monthly Magazine.* https://www.golfmonthly.com/features/the-game/who-coaches-tiger-woods-162053

2. Reporter, Guardian Staff. (2021, August 30). Angelo Dundee at 100: The calm heart of Muhammad Ali's boxing career. *The Guardian.* https://www.theguardian.com/sport/2021/aug/30/angelo-dundee-muhammad-ali-trainer-boxing

3. Hamlin, Robert G. (2009, February 1). Toward a profession of coaching? A definitional examination of "coaching," "organization development," and "human resource development." *ResearchOnline.* https://doi.org/10.24384/IJEBCM

4. Gray, David E. (2006, December). Executive coaching: Towards a dynamic alliance of psychotherapy and transformative learning processes. *Management Learning* 37(4): 475–497. https://doi.org/10.1177/1350507606070221

5. Hwang, Chan Young, Kang, Seung-Wan, and Choi, Suk Bong. (2023, March 28). Coaching leadership and creative performance: A serial mediation model of psychological empowerment and constructive voice behavior. *Frontiers in Psychology.* Frontiers Media. https://doi.org/10.3389/fpsyg.2023.1077594

Chapter 20

1. Clark, Ryan. (2023, August 7). Mike Vrabel gets it. *Twitter.* https://x.com/Realrclark25/status/1688637183593168896?s=20

2. Robinson, Charles. (2023, August 10). Mike Vrabel tapping assistant Terrell Williams to lead the Titans on Saturday is key moment in NFL

coaching. *Yahoo Sports.* https://sports.yahoo.com/mike-vrabel-tapping-assistant-terrell-williams-to-lead-the-titans-on-saturday-is-key-moment-in-nfl-coaching-020606305.html

3. Kahneman, Daniel, and Tversky, Amos. (1979, March). Prospect theory: An analysis of decision under risk. *Econometrica* 47(2): 263. https://doi.org/10.2307/1914185

4. Cranston, Susie, and Keller, Scott. (2013, January 1). Increasing the "meaning quotient" of work. McKinsey & Company. https://www.mckinsey.com/capabilities/people-and-organizational-performance/our-insights/increasing-the-meaning-quotient-of-work

5. Cranston, Susie, and Keller, Scott. (2013, January 1). Increasing the "meaning quotient" of work. McKinsey & Company. https://www.mckinsey.com/capabilities/people-and-organizational-performance/our-insights/increasing-the-meaning-quotient-of-work

Chapter 21

1. Terrell Owens on Eagles breakup: Everybody knows it really wasn't my fault. (2016, December 2). *CBSSports.com.* https://www.cbssports.com/nfl/news/terrell-owens-on-eagles-breakup-everybody-knows-it-really-wasnt-my-fault/

2. *Any Given Sunday.* (n.d.). *IMDb.* https://www.imdb.com/title/tt0146838/characters/nm0000199

3. An in-depth guide to team effectiveness. (2023, August 7). Managing Life at Work. https://managinglifeatwork.com/team-effectiveness/

4. Army team building. (2015, October). Army Techniques Publication. https://armypubs.army.mil/epubs/DR_pubs/DR_a/pdf/web/atp6_22x6%20FINAL.pdf

5. How the Navy's "hell week" reveals who has what it takes to be a SEAL. (2021, January 21). Navy SEALs. https://navyseals.com/5436/how-the-navys-hell-week-reveals-who-has-what-it-takes-to-be-a-seal/

Chapter 22

1. Leiker, Emily. (2021, June 11). Lore and impact of Michael Jordan's 1997 "Flu Game" still relevant 24 years later. *USA Today.* https://www.usatoday.com/story/sports/nba/2021/06/11/michael-jordan-flu-game-24th-anniversary/7652703002/

2. Carucci, Ron. (2020, November 23). How to actually encourage employee accountability. *Harvard Business Review.* https://hbr.org/2020/11/how-to-actually-encourage-employee-accountability

3. Harter, Jim. (2023, July 21). U.S. employee engagement rises following wild 2020. *Gallup.com*. https://www.gallup.com/workplace/330017/employee-engagement-rises-following-wild-2020.aspx

4. Walsh, Bill, Jamison, Steve, and Walsh, Craig. (2009). *The score takes care of itself*. Penguin.

5. Bill Walsh Standards of Performance. (2020, March 14). *Football Toolbox*. https://footballtoolbox.net/program-building/hall-of-fame-coachs-standards-of-performance

6. Tran, Sang Kim Tran. GOOGLE: A reflection of culture, leader, and management. (2017, December 1). *International Journal of Corporate Social Responsibility*. Springer Nature. https://doi.org/10.1186/s40991-017-0021-0

7. Muna, Farid A., and Zennie, Ziad A. (2010, January 1). *Styles of emotionally intelligent leaders*. Palgrave Macmillan UK eBooks. https://doi.org/10.1057/9781137104649_8

Chapter 23

1. Bradberry, Travis. (2023). *Emotional intelligence habits*. TalentSmart.

2. Duckworth, Angela. (2016). *Grit*. Simon and Schuster.

3. McRaven, Admiral William H. (2023). *The wisdom of the bullfrog*. Hachette UK.

Chapter 24

1. Rock, David. (2019, March 19). Why diverse teams are smarter. *Harvard Business Review*. https://hbr.org/2016/11/why-diverse-teams-are-smarter

2. Lorenzo, Rocío, Voigt, Nicole, Tsusaka, Miki, Krentz, Matt, and Abouzahr, Katie. (2023, January 23). How diverse leadership teams boost innovation. BCG Global. https://www.bcg.com/publications/2018/how-diverse-leadership-teams-boost-innovation

3. Margaret Hamilton—NASA science. (n.d.). https://science.nasa.gov/people/margaret-hamilton/

4. Charan, Ram, Barton, Dominic, and Carey, Dennis. (2018). *Talent wins*. Harvard Business Press.

Chapter 25

1. Pfau, Bruce N. (2017, November 30). How an accounting firm convinced its employees they could change the world. *Harvard Business*

Review. https://hbr.org/2015/10/how-an-accounting-firm-convinced-its-employees-they-could-change-the-world

2. Ignatius, Adi. (2016, November 3). How Indra Nooyi turned design thinking into strategy: An interview with PepsiCo's CEO. *Harvard Business Review.* https://hbr.org/2015/09/how-indra-nooyi-turned-design-thinking-into-strategy

3. Ignatius, Adi. (2016, November 3). How Indra Nooyi turned design thinking into strategy: An interview with PepsiCo's CEO. *Harvard Business Review.* https://hbr.org/2015/09/how-indra-nooyi-turned-design-thinking-into-strategy

4. Platts, Chris. (2018, September 21). How to get cultural fit right. *People Management* magazine. https://www.peoplemanagement.co.uk/article/1746133/how-to-get-cultural-fit-right

5. The Deloitte Global 2023 Gen Z and Millennial Survey. (2023, July 21). Deloitte. https://www.deloitte.com/global/en/issues/work/content/genzmillennialsurvey.html

6. EY Beacon Institute. The business case for purpose. (2015). *Harvard Business Review Analytic Services Report.* https://assets.ey.com/content/dam/ey-sites/ey-com/en_gl/topics/digital/ey-the-business-case-for-purpose.pdf

7. Job security and meaningful work in high demand for today's workforce. (n.d.). *Net Impact.* https://netimpact.org/about/press-releases/job-security-and-meaningful-work-in-high-demand-for-todays-workforce

8. From ambition to action: How to attain purpose-led transformation. (2022). Ernst & Young. https://assets.ey.com/content/dam/ey-sites/ey-com/en_uk/topics/workforce/how-to-attain-purpose-led-transformation.pdf

9. Purpose: Shifting from why to how. (2020, April 22). McKinsey & Company. https://www.mckinsey.com/capabilities/people-and-organizational-performance/our-insights/purpose-shifting-from-why-to-how

10. The heart of business with Hubert Joly. (n.d.). Yale School of Management. https://som.yale.edu/blog/the-heart-of-business-with-hubert-joly

11. Sinek, Simon. (2011). *Start with why.* Penguin.

Chapter 27

1. Rogers, Suzi. (2017, February 17). This study reveals the 5 biggest regrets people have before they die by John-Paul Iwuoha. American Recruiters. https://www.americanrecruiters.com/2017/02/17/study-reveals-5-biggest-regrets-people-die-john-paul-iwuoha/

2. Wiederman, Michael W. (2015, March 5). Mortal thoughts. *Scientific American*. Springer Nature. https://doi.org/10.1038/scientificamerican-secrets0315-58

3. The bright side of death: Awareness of mortality can result in positive behaviors. (2012, April 12). *ScienceDaily*. https://www.sciencedaily.com/releases/2012/04/120430164359.htm

4. Shpancer, Noam. (2021, May 12). The life benefits of contemplating death. *Psychology Today*. https://www.psychologytoday.com/intl/blog/insight-therapy/202105/the-life-benefits-contemplating-death

Acknowledgments

To MY WONDERFUL parents, I offer my deepest gratitude and respect. As time passes and I grow older, I realize just how extremely fortunate I am. Mom, your unwavering support and the unconditional love you provide are admirable and one of the greatest gifts I have received. Dad, I want to thank you for being the first transformational leader I ever saw in action, and your influence lives on through me each and every day.

I am extremely grateful for the army of people who have been gracious enough to give their time and energy to help bring this book to life. To my wonderful publishing partner at Wiley, thank you for giving me the platform to continually express my ideas and insights. Most importantly, thank you for believing in me and for your continued support. I would like to personally acknowledge Victoria Savanh, Trinity Crompton, Michelle Hacker, Shannon Vargo, Julie Kerr, Jason Boulay, and Katie Kotchman.

I would like to extend my sincere gratitude to my team for its invaluable support, which laid the groundwork for blocking off the time to write this book in the first place.

I am extremely grateful to my wife, Aubry, for her steadfast support and understanding when writing deadlines begin to consume my every thought. You are my greatest supporter, and your selflessness in the face of my often chaotic schedule is truly remarkable.

Last but not least, I want to thank every leader who took time out of their busy schedule to speak with me about this book or provide feedback by reading early drafts. And this book would not be possible without the extraordinary clients I am so fortunate to work with.

About the Author

Matt Mayberry is an internationally acclaimed keynote speaker and one of the world's foremost thought leaders on leadership development and organizational culture. His insights on leadership, culture, and organizational performance have appeared in publications such as *Forbes*; *Fortune*; *Business Insider*; *Harvard Business Review*; *Entrepreneur*; *Fox Business, Inc. Magazine*; ABC; ESPN; and many more major media outlets.

Mayberry also serves as a trusted adviser to many of the world's most prestigious organizations, with clients that include JP Morgan Chase, Allstate Insurance, AT&T, DuPont, OptumRX, Mack Trucks, Fifth Third Bank, and the Federal Bureau of Investigation (FBI), to name a few.

Global Gurus named him one of the world's top 30 thought leaders on leadership, and his leadership and workplace culture training programs were among the top 10.

Mayberry's journey to success began on the football field. He was a prominent athlete with the Indiana Hoosiers, and later the Chicago Bears, but an injury he sustained during his first NFL game cut his career short. Still, the invaluable lessons learned on the field and from influential coaches are foundational to his insights on leadership, excellence, teamwork, and culture.

Mayberry is the author of the *Wall Street Journal* bestseller *Culture Is the Way* (2023) and *Winning Plays* (2016). Residing in Chicago, Illinois, his work continues inspiring and transforming leadership practices and team dynamics across the globe.

Speaking

Matt Mayberry has become one of the world's most sought-after speakers due to his thought leadership, dynamic, and high-energy keynote presentations. His powerful insights into organizational culture, leadership, peak performance, and teamwork captivate global audiences, ranging from small executive teams to conferences with up to 12,000 attendees.

With infectious energy and masterful storytelling, Matt combines lessons learned as a world-class athlete and insight gleaned from advising some of today's most successful organizations. Experience the impact of his unique blend of real-world experience and practical knowledge to make your next event unforgettable.

The same preparation and dedication to mastery that catapulted him as an athlete have served as a guiding force behind every speech, ensuring superior impact. This level of excellence drives his commitment to ensure each and every keynote presentation is relevant, specific, and deeply inspiring.

To invite Matt to speak at your next event or meeting, please visit https://mattmayberryonline.com or send an email to Matt at info@mattmayberryonline.com. Don't miss this opportunity to bring one of the world's most sought-after keynote speakers to your audience.

Index